Celebrating 77 with Childhood Memories

of Korean War on Its 70th Anniversary

Celebrating 77 with Childhood Memories
of Korean War on Its 70th Anniversary

First Printing | Dec 19. 2020.
Author | Kyunggi Girls' High School, Class of 1963
Editor | Yoon-kyung Lee
Edition Staff | Young Choi, Youngja M. Chon, Shin hyun Chun,
　　　　　　　　Jung-yoon Lee, Kyung-soon Lee, Jungsoon Ryu,
　　　　　　　　Jung-im Yum

Administrative Staff | Kil-sook Cho, Yang-ja Choi, Yong-won Kim,
　　　　　　　　　　　　Hyun-pyo Lee, Bong-hee Park, Hee-won Shin
Cover Image | Si-un Kim

ISBN | 9798580689302

www.amazon.com
© Kyunggi Girls' High School, Class of 1963, 2020

Celebrating 77 with Childhood Memories
of Korean War on Its 70th Anniversary

Kyunggi Girls' High School
Class of 1963
(51st Graduating Class)

Contents

Foreword

A celebration was in order - our high school classmates were about to turn 77 years young - and we thought we had a plan to convene us all together. But what they say about best-laid plans turned out to be true. Amid a global pandemic and confined to our homes, we went digital.

More than 220 classmates from all around the world joined the Internet messaging system as soon as it was set up. We even ventured into video conferencing, which many of us had thought was just for special professional groups.

It just so happened that it was also the time to commemorate the 70th Anniversary of the Korean War, 6.25, which broke out on 25th of June, 1950.

One of us shared her 6.25 memory, triggering a flood of similar stories. Some fragmentary episodes were vaguely remembered, some vividly, but each memory carried with it a personal truth, a piece of life. To preserve these memories, we agreed to capture them in writing.

Furthermore, we realized the extent to which our childhood memories shaped our lives. So, we also wrote our life stories of the past 70 years since the war. What happened to the child who once lived in a refugee tent? What happened to the scared little girl who once clung onto the roof of a refugee train?

And thus, this book came to be. Sixty five essays were collected in a short period of time, beginning with childhood memories of the war, continuing with stories of our youth and adulthood, and spanning across the world as we carried our stories, our roots, with us to the various places where we made our homes.

We hope that in these stories, readers may recognize the uniqueness of those times that our generation lived through, and through this tapestry of memories, we hope, in some small way, to bring history further to life.

We're profoundly indebted to those who have contributed these essays and to families and friends for their support and encouragement. We're grateful to Young Choi, Shin-hyun Chun, Youngja Chon, Jung-yoon Lee, Kyung-soon Lee, Jungsoon Ryu, Jung-im Yum for serving as editors, and also to Kil-sook Cho, Yang-ja Choi, Yong-won Kim, Hyun-pyo Lee, Bong-hee Park, and Hee-won Shin for their dedicated hands-on editorial work. A deep appreciation is also for Si-un Kim for her artwork on the cover design.

Dr. Yoon-kyung Lee
President, Class of 1963
of Kyunggi Girls' High School
October 7, 2020

A Festival Stage

Ki-Han Sohng

The graduates of Class of 1963, Kyunggi Girls' High School published 'In celebration of the 77th anniversary of their life and in commemoration of 6.25.' One of the subtitles of the book is 'on the Road Together: #3', so this time it is their third book. It seems like an easy task for a group to come together and weave their stories into a book, but it is by no means so. This is because in order for this to be possible, they must know each other and there should be a common culture or memories they can share.

What has helped the Kyunggi graduates to form into a tight group is that they are high school alumni. In addition, they have shared experiences of war when they were six or seven years old. War always remains an original experience for generations who have experienced it.

The class of 1963 graduates of Kyunggi Girls' High School are the generation who directly experienced the war. Therefore, the vivid things that they have gone through at the time must have left deep imprints on them.

This book is a collection of their experiences. It can

be said that in this book one dimension of our modern history has been vividly recorded. One of the values of this book is that it brought to surface what had been left dormant for a long time. Such restoration alone may be of sufficient historical value. Moreover, the painful emotional trauma is not confined only to those of the past, but it also gives us in the present a message of warming. That's where its significance lies.

In addition, this book portrays their personal life, and the way they run their daily lives from various angles. The trivialities of their daily routines and their sentiments are being revealed before us in many layers. This is also a case of universal value in that it is not only their own sentiments, but it can also be incorporated into ours.

'In celebration of the 77th anniversary of their life and the commemoration of 6.25' are revived memories of the past and daily lives of the present in two layers. The layers reject uniformity. Even though they are the same age, their experiences are diverse, and the way they live in the present life is also diverse. This book is a brilliant and colorful collection of writings created by this diversity. For that reason, it stands tall not only just in the past, but it stands tall also in the present. On the other hand, as the daily life of the present communicates with the past, the layers of life can expand in various ways. It is difficult to say that this book is limited to the experiences of one particular group. This is because the diversity of the past and that of the present are expressed as diverse as a fan in the languages of various experiences. And their experiences are sublimated to ours as they create a fun festival. As we participate in this festival space together, it is that we are sharing their past memories and also actively participating in the present life that they enjoy.

In that universal zone of experiences and dialogues, their past as well as their present, their memories and their experiences are no more theirs alone, but become ours to share. That is the great significance this book offers.

Dr. Ki-Han, Sohng is a professor of Korean Literature at Daejeon University.

Taking the Pen in Their Hands

Ki-Moon Lee

<From Chosun Ilbo, Jan. 16, 2021>

Turning 77, Kyunggi Girls' High School Classmates picked up their pens instead of throwing a big party. They wrote their childhood memories of the Korean War: the stories of the textbook that was never read, the wristwatch that father gave away to the North Korean soldier to save his life, the song 'the Moonlit Night in Shilla' that the child heard when she lost her mother – the mementos of intense memories. They say in unison: the childhood experiences of the war shaped our lives, and we are grateful to have survived.

"2020년 희수를 맞은 경기여고 동창들이 기념 잔치를 하는 대신 펜을 들었다. 일곱 살 적 겪은 한국 전쟁의 기억을 묶었다. 한 번도 읽지 못한 교과서, 아버지가 생존의 대가로 인민군에게 건넨 손목시계, 엄마를 잃어버릴 때 들렸던 노래 '신라의 달밤' 등 강렬했던 기억의 증표들을 풀어놓는다. 그들은 입을 모아 말한다. 어린 날의 전쟁이 삶에 영향을 줬고, 살아있는 것에 감사한다고."

Ki-Moon Lee is a newspaper journalist for Chosun Ilbo, Seoul, Korea.

Part 1. Childhood Memories of Korean War

We start this part with a silo by Yukdang Choi Name-son, which he wrote in September of 1950, after losing his eldest   daughter, who, leaving behind her six children, had been murdered by the North Korean soldiers.

What follows are the stories of our own 6.25 memories. Although the episodes might have happened in different circumstances, we realize that they are shared experiences with a deep impact, and making the sharing ever more meaningful. So, here we go.

1.   No Title-14 (Sept. 1950)

Yuktang Choi Nam-son (Grandfather of 최동주)

Translated by Yer-ae K. Choi (김여애)

For forty-two years you lived
    a life of beauty and purity.
Your six children whom you loved so much
    are still here,
But you, who held them under your wings,
    are here no more.

The poisonous arrow has found you
    as its mark.
As if aware that stains show up better
    against white,
The sign of evil times has chosen you
    as its target.

Grief does not end the way
    tear marks dry.
I'll weep to my heart's content,
    beating on my chest.
Silencing a father's love, can one act
    as if reason has returned?

2. The Remains of War Memories

Young Choi (최 영)

A piece of tapestry scattered with sundry hues and fragmented patterns resurrects memories from the Korean War. My experience's vivid colors and shapes are mingled with misty figures from the stories I have heard. One thing I can say with confidence, though, is that the root of all my anxiety, dread, and obsessions can be traced back to this war.

The Korean War broke out on June 25, 1950, when I was six years old. It was a Sunday. I distinctly remember how the atmosphere, loaded with dread and fear, permeated the entire household. Whispering rumors that lingered in the air over the past couple of months had finally become a reality.

The North Korean communist soldiers who showed up at our house with submachine guns were my introduction to the ugly face of war. They surprised each household wildly and ferociously searching for men. My father and uncles locked themselves in the cellar and attic of our neighbor's house. One day the soldiers came and fired into the air, threatening us to reveal my father's hiding place; luckily, they were never discovered. The kids could no longer play in the alley;

13

instead, we had to be on the lookout for soldiers with guns.

From mid-September, the B-28 and B-29 bomber attacks escalated fiercely. We moved to an air-raid shelter cave on a nearby hillside. At night, my younger brother and I fascinatingly watched the red lights from the bombers sparkling in the dark sky.

While most of us were trying our best to endure this devastating new life, others started to emerge conspicuously. One such woman was a peddler with a pockmarked face, who had spent most of her life selling household utensils. When the war broke out, she was transformed into a leader of a communist group of women, and began to exercise her power. Her long-lost husband had also reemerged as a high-ranking communist party member. The days of glory, though, were brief. Her husband was forced to retreat back to the North when the UN troops regained Seoul. He once again deserted his wife and the baby boy.

The days of liberation from communist rule were terminated when the Chinese Red Army joined the North Korean Communist military, forcing the UN forces and the Korea Army to retreat to the South. My family also joined the hundreds of thousands of refugees heading South.

After we settled in Daegu, I experienced a different facet of the war. In Daegu, I met American soldiers, both white and black. Along with other foreign soldiers from various countries, their presence manifested an international dimension of this war.

One summer evening, an American soldier entered our house through the open gate. The great-grandmother in her eighties instantly realized why he was there. In our place there were only women, except for my 4 year old brother. To protect us, she rushed at him brandishing her broom to push him out. He had a pistol on him. Something horrific could happen at any moment. My brother and I waited helplessly for something dramatic to happen. The soldier looked down, smilingly at the old woman who could barely reach his waist. He retreated back toward the gate and left. Nothing happened. But the sense of impending dread stemming from that moment remained with me for a long time.

I began attending school in Daegu. The makeshift classrooms were created with army tents, equipped only with blackboards. Every day when I went to school, I brought with me a drawing pad and a cushion for my chair. One memorable day, a small box filled with stationery was delivered to our class. It was a gift from the Americans. The colors of pencils and crayons were so beautiful and alluring that they kindled a sense of curiosity in me and a yearning to learn beyond what I had known. In retrospect, this classroom was the place where my initiation into the bigger and wider world had started.

After a year, my family moved to Busan to join my father. My school here was located on the slope of Gumjong Mountain. I spent more time wandering around the mountainside than staying in the classroom. During the summer vacation, we had the assignment to fill matchboxes with grass seeds to be exported to the U.S.

While in Daegu, I only saw everyday life's facade despite our genuine struggle for survival. In Busan, I became aware of how people were grappling under the pressures of an ongoing war. The suburban district of Dongrae, where we settled, was a peaceful resort area with hot springs. Refugees were pouring into this area because it was the furthest away from the front line where the war relentlessly forged on.

Some people made a show of conspicuous consumption. People could easily procure foreign goods--imported or smuggled--and relief goods. Among this melange of exotic imports were foreign drinks that I tasted for the first time at a classmate's home. Her family was running an orphanage that received an abundance of relief goods primarily from the U.S. The taste of foreign foods captivated me more than the colorful crayons, luring me into newfound curiosity about foreign lands.

Our playground was the mountain road. Whenever the army trucks approached, we had to disperse up and down the street and waited until the dust settled before resuming our play. The soldiers stuck three branches in their helmets. We waved to them as they headed to the front lines. They looked very young as if they were fresh out of high school.

We were approaching the third year of the war, and the impact of combat pervaded profoundly into everyday lives. The anxious, restless, sad atmosphere dominated us, and the unruly, rude, and uncouth behaviors of war were hardly contained.

The armistice of the Korean War was signed on July 27, 1953. My family returned to Seoul after three years of refugee life. The shock and trauma of the war were entrenched deep within me and resurfaced in the form of nightmares. With slight variations, the nightmares were predominantly about helplessly losing siblings during the evacuation from Seoul. The combination of reality and prevalent children's books about losing one's parents or siblings had a significant impact on my psyche.

On rainy days, the ruins and debris from the houses and buildings exude a haunting ambiance. There were rumors that skeletons had been excavated in the cellars. In the discarded dugouts on the hillside of Inwang Mountain nearby my school lived beggars and lepers. Another kind of rumor was that they kidnapped small children. Whenever we walked on the streets in downtown Seoul, we encountered disabled soldiers and civilians. The wounded people who had lost arms, legs, and other body parts during the war were so frightening to me that I wanted to run away from them.

Though I had survived through the Korean War, sinister memories have permeated my mind and engraved indelible marks upon my character. The trauma from being a refugee has manifested in a nomadic inability to rest leisurely in any one location and the habit of collecting and hoarding books, souvenirs, remembrances, and letters. None of which can be disassociated from my war experience.

Dr. Young Choi is a professor emerita at Ewha Womans University. She taught English and American Literature for 31 years.

3.   A Child in Refuge Camp

Gae Tack Han (양계택)

< This essay first appeared in 'Our Roots, Our Lives: Glimpses of Faith and Life From Black and Asian Canadian Women', The United Church Publishing House. 2003.>

"Mom, I'm going out!"

I ran outside to the South Korean soldiers' barracks. I didn't like staying in the tent. It was dark and stuffy, a noisy place with too many people in it. I wanted to get away. Camping is not fun if you have to do it every day, the way we had been doing for months. I wished my family lived in a house again, not in this refugee camp. Here we were living in a tent just like soldiers. But were not soldiers. We were just ordinary people running away from war, trying to survive.

A few us kids used to get over to the barracks now and then to sing. The South Korean soldiers enjoyed listening to North Korean songs, especially the one about General Kim Il Sung. I often wondered why they wanted to hear about an enemy general. Perhaps they found it amusing to see little children singing propaganda songs. Sometimes they would try to sing with us: we had to teach them how.

Our parents worried when we went out to play with the soldiers. These soldiers often carried us on their shoulders. The parents were not happy about this at all, but they did not know what to do about it since they were afraid of the soldiers. Sometimes the soldiers would give us snacks. This made the parents particularly uneasy, because war made every gesture, however kindly meant, dangerously political. In retrospect, I am sure that the soldiers played with us out of pity or, at worst, to gain some information through us. But mostly I recall having lots of fun with the other kids from this refugee camp located on the immediate border between North and South Korea. Even today I can still remember some of the games we played, and sing by heart some of the songs we sang.

Our time in the refugee camp left a much deeper scar on my mother. Her experiences there, of being left without a "home," made her feel "uprooted" for a long time afterwards. Even today, more than 50 years later, she still talks about how difficult it was living with four families in one army tent. "We had a wood-or was it charcoal?-stove in the middle of the tent. Each family was assigned their tiny corner of the tent where they ate their meals on the floor. We had to take turns cooking. Whenever any of cooked anything, however, it always smelt and tasted delicious. Maybe it was because we didn't have much to eat most of the time." We had so little, in fact, that Mother used to wake up early in the morning to walk a long way to the cabbage fields to pick up the leftover leaves from the harvest. She would then walk back to the camp, boil the leaves to make a special dish called *searaegi*, which she then sold at the market. How hard this must have been for someone whose family used to own large tracts of land near Pyongyang before the land was appropriated by the Communist regime after World War II, I cannot even begin to imagine.

One day, while at her usual "stand" at the market, she heard astonished voices crying, "How dare you sit on the street selling that stuff!" It was farmers who had come from my grandfather's farm further north. They could not believe their eyes. It was shocking for them to see my mother, the daughter of a large landowner, trying to sell her pitiful cabbage dish at the public market. But my mother was happy to see them again.

"How lovely to meet you here again in the South," she greeted them cheerfully. "How are you? How is your family?" I think those farmers felt closer to my mother then, and therefore to us, than they had ever felt before. We were now all in the same boat, uprooted people searching for a home. Of course, the war eventually ended, and we ended up living in a

21

house in Seoul, but I doubt that that house was ever really "home" to my mother, after her experience in the refugee camp and at the market.

My mother is now 86. Sometimes she forgets what is happening around her. Nowadays, I am careful not to remind her of the refugee camp and all the painful experiences of the past. Once in a while, though, she herself would start telling stories from that difficult period. She remembers many details quite vividly. I always listen attentively, because I am still trying to understand her journey-and mine. I often reflect on the concept of "roots" and how the different places I lived at various times have nourished my sense of belonging. My five siblings and I have carried our "roots" from North Korea to South Korea, and then to Canada or the United States at different times. We have been in North America now for over 40 years.

What I have learned about "roots" and the sense of belonging is that you can plant things in your heart, not just in the soil. If you feel rooted in your heart, then it does not matter where you live. Maybe our children will feel they have similar "roots," but again, maybe not. All the same, I think it is important that they have some concept of "home," even if it is a space in their heart, a space where they can always return, there to feel safe and loved.

Gae T. Han is a program staff person at Ethnic Ministries, the United Church of Canada. As a member of the Toronto Korean United Church since the late 1960s, she is committed to the Christian faith formation of children and youth and to empowering the leadership of racial ethnic minority women.

4.   My First Unread Textbooks

Min-sook Kang (강민숙)

April – June 1950

When I turned six years old, I was finally able to go to school, just like my older brother. My mother made a pink polka-dot dress with puff sleeves and a pleated neck with a white frill. On the opening day of school, my mother pinned a white handkerchief on my dress on the left side and took me there. In the first few days of school, all we did was to form straight class lines, practice standing at attention, and giving salutes in the schoolyard.

I was able to go to school by myself a few days later. I remember the time when I wanted to show off my school backpack. Everything in the bag spilled on the playground when I knelt, and the unused pencils and notebooks tumbled out of it to the ground. I must have forgotten to lock it after showing them off to my friends.

Since then, I went to school without the backpack, only carrying my shoe pouch. Finally, we received two textbooks that we had been waiting for. My schoolteacher said we would get two more books later. I put those books in my shoe pouch and came home, swinging it happily. The next school day, my mom wouldn't let me go to school, however. I wanted to study with my new textbooks and my carefully sharpened pencils, but she wouldn't allow me to go. I was anxious to get my two other books, too, but she said that war had broken out. I didn't know what "war" meant. I didn't realize at the time that I wouldn't be able to go to school for the next two and a half years. I still feel sad thinking about my first unread textbooks.

July – September 1950

Some children in the neighborhood said they were going to school, but my mother still wouldn't allow me to go. The school kids sang many songs, and I learned to sing along with them. But my grandmother and mom didn't want me to sing those songs, either. I couldn't understand why.

There weren't any adult men around the house: my father, uncles, and cousins; they all disappeared. When I got bored, I often went to jongno street by myself to watch street parades. Many enthusiastic people were carrying pickets and signs with big drawings of mustached Stalin and Mao Zedong, marching toward Dongdaemoon. Our Grandfather passed away in February of that year, so we had a Sangchung (memorial table) on the main floor. We were supposed to prepare food for the memorial every morning and evening. One day I found my mom sobbing because she couldn't find food to put on the memorial table because of the war.

September 20-26, 1950

When our National army tried to recapture Seoul, the bombing became severe. Our house in Jongno had a cement cellar underneath the main floor. We used it as a shelter and hid there for several days with our neighbors. We grabbed our belongings and spread blankets on the floor. Even during the day, we had to use candles because it was so dark in the cellar.

One day, when the sun was still up, there was a thunderous noise. Wind and dirt came pouring in, blocking the door and blowing out all the candles. My mother immediately covered my brothers and me with blankets, and all we could hear was screaming. After a moment, everything quieted down. There was no fire or smoke because fortunately the bomb that landed in our neighborhood didn't explode. Everyone said that it was my Grandfather's faith that saved us; he was a profoundly religious man. Before the war, I remember following Grandfather to Taegosa Temple (Jogyesa Temple) and nearby Pagoda Park often.

September 27-30, 1950

On both sides of Cheonggyecheon, where Gwanggyo Bridge is visible, there were many tile-roofed houses. Children often played by the roadside. If the weather was good and didn't rain, the sandy streambed along Cheonggyecheon exposed an area like a Ssireum (Korean wrestling) arena. Cheonggyechoen made an excellent playground for children with clear water.

When our National army tried to recapture Seoul, the airial bombings were heavy. The streets from Kwangwhamoon to Jongno were burning. Refugees escaped from the burning neighborhood filled both sides of Cheonggyecheon. The bomb landed on our house just two days before, and it was also burning.

October 1950 – January 1951

We didn't know where my father was, and we didn't have a house in Seoul because our house caught fire when the bomb hit. We walked all the way to my mom's parents' home in Yeoju. The war was getting worse. The weather was getting cold, but men still had to serve in the national army. Every day, I saw men in cotton-padded pants, jackets, and a hat or muffler covering their heads, endlessly passing by from the north to south of Yeoju.

The villagers said that we also had to go south to

escape from the war. So our family put bags of rice, side dishes, blankets, and bowls into an ox-drawn wagon. My great-grandmother, who was over 80 years old, and my big brother, who had recently injured his leg, stayed behind at the house. My mother protested in tears saying that she would stay at home with them, but Grandfather said sternly that she needed to care for the three other children

My mother was just 30 years old at the time, and my big brother was nine. Mom and my aunt carried my baby brother and my three-year-old younger brother, each on their backs, and I walked. We walked for more than 15 days, finding a shelter to cook and sleep in the evenings.

One day we heard the good news that our troops had moved north of the 38th parallel. We turned around and walked back to my Grandfather's house. My great-grandmother and brother greeted us, and we hugged each other and wept for joy. Despite the chaos and hardship, the village remained peaceful the rest of the war.

September 1952

A long-awaited letter finally came from my father. Now my family was about to go to Busan to meet him. I was so happy that I wanted to run outside and shout to the world that I would finally go see my father. I was so glad I could fly. Mom bought a train ticket for my big brother to Busan but no ticket for me. Whenever the conductor inspected tickets, I had to hide under the seat or curl into a ball. Mom bought me a roll of Gimbap, but I was so disappointed with it. There was only rice inside, no fillings. Since there were stains of red pepper on both ends of gimbap, I thought there were gimchi fillings inside.

We arrived at Busan station in the middle of the night, and my father's friend, whom we met on the train, guided us to Choryang, where my father was supposed to be waiting for us. He had a relative in Choryang, and I'm still grateful for their generosity in having us and serving us dinner late at night.

The next day, we followed my father's instructions in his letter and went near Choryang train station, looking for a two-story red brick house. There was a two-story, red-brick warehouse in the refugee neighborhood. We continued looking, not realizing that the warehouse was what my father meant, but there was no other brick house nearby. They partitioned the inside of the brick warehouse into several rooms. I wasn't old enough to understand, then, but I can imagine now how very disappointed my mother and aunt must have been to see the warehouse. Didn't my mom dream of a red brick house, with a chimney and fireplace, fit for a prince and princess from a fairy tale? My parents have now passed away, and I miss them all the more when I think back on the war. My humorous aunt and I reminisce about many war stories when we meet. The "red brick two-story house" has become one of our favorite topics.

I'm just grateful that now we are in a peaceful place and can share our stories with fond memories.

Min-sook Kang is an Illinois registered nurse, and also a Korean Essay Debut Essayist.

5.   Shadows of War

Hyun-pyo Lee (이현표)

I had a big surgery in my twenties. When I woke up from anesthesia, my family told me I was sobbing uncontrollably during the surgery. I wasn't crying from pain or terror - I must have been crying subconsciously. I still think about it sometimes. Perhaps my subconscious had traveled to the worst memory of my life and was crying for that. I still remember it so vividly - I was only six, wailing at a truck leaving me behind.

When UN troops retreated from Seoul in January 1951, my family immediately left Seoul away from the North Korean army. My parents decided to leave me and my older sister, six and nine years old, behind to take care of my grandmother, who had been ill and was unable to move. I have four brothers and three older sisters, and an infant sister who was born just as the war began. In retrospect, they probably figured it would be safer to leave younger ones behind in the midst of war rather than teenage daughters.

The six-year-old me cried my heart out watching the truck leave with my family.

It is only recently that I finally asked my second oldest sister - seven years older than me - where they went in the truck. She told me they only went as far as Suwon in that truck, just outside Seoul, then had to walk roughly 185 miles all the way to Daegu. They then made their way to Busan, where there is a temple for the progenitors of my mother's aristocratic family. To get food, I heard that my father sold the land-price securities he held at throwaway price. As the only son of one of the wealthiest families in Korea, my father had received from the government in exchange for acres and acres of inherited family land, but they had turned nearly worthless overnight.

My sister and I would lay on the wooden floor of the central hall, humming the songs we overheard the North Korean soldiers were singing, or watch neighbors taking food from our pantry room from the bedroom window. Our maid, Sukja, disappeared after meeting a North Korean soldier.

In the meantime, while we were left alone in Seoul, my nine-year-old sister somehow got me enrolled in the nearby elementary school. If it wasn't my sister, I wouldn't have been able to start school with my age group.

Seoul was reclaimed in March 15, 1951, about 70 days after the retreat. Soon after that my older brother, who was seventeen at the time, came home with loads of chocolate and sausages. He'd followed the US army as a Scout volunteer when Seoul was reclaimed so he could come check on us. Not long after that my oldest brother came for us, and we took the train to Busan to be reunited with the family.

My mother, who was a wonderful cook who'd hosted fabulous parties for decades for our family, set up a donut shop and made twisty doughnuts that resembled taraegwa, a traditional fried braided snack that were served on ceremonious rituals. We branded them "Seoul Doughnuts" and they literally sold like hot cakes until the chimney of our wooden shack burned down. Even I lent a hand when making the twisty doughnuts. When I later got married, I'd often make my two sons twisty doughnuts for snack time.

After the Armistice agreement we returned home to Seoul. I'd hardly been to school - I remember kids making fun of me for getting a zero score on my first test. But at least I was in my proper school year. Thanks to my sister.

Somewhere in my subconscious the shadows of war must have a grip on my soul but I was never even aware of it. Same thing happened to my oldest sister.

During the war, my maternal grandfather Jung Inbo – regarded as one of the greatest philosophers and historians of the era – was abducted to North Korea. When the incident occurred my oldest sister was taking care of him. She still speaks of the abduction in her hallucinations as if she was living it over and over again. She is now in the hospital, nearing ninety, slipping in and out of consciousness. When her mind goes away, she grabs my second oldest sister's hand and says things that hardly make sense. "My ring is too big! Let's swap my ring with your smaller diamond to give him!" When my grandfather was forcibly taken by the North Korean soldier, she must have wanted to bribe the soldier with jewels so he'd let our grandfather go. This must have been the most terrifying, traumatizing experience of her life, which left an indelible mark on her mind. Her old soul is so filled with the ardent desire to be given a second chance to save our grandfather that she slips back into that time whenever her consciousness loses grip on reality. Those of us who can only guess at her life-long grief check her fingers for her ring every time we visit her.

It was in my forties that I began learning to sew traditional Hanbok from my mother, who was named a Living National Treasure for her traditional dressmaking skills. I loved our quiet times together, sitting side by side, sewing and chatting. During all that time we spent together I never asked, and she never talked about the war. Probably because it's such a horrid memory and none of us wanted to relive it. It's a pity that I'm only curious now, after she has passed.

Looking back, it's all a miracle. Our entire family survived - father, mother, and all nine brothers and sisters. We even received our education.

But who could ever resolve these profound, ghastly scars caused by our own people!

Hyun P. Lee Served as an education professional in National Board of Education Evaluation of Korea, and served two middle schools (Dong-jak and Pung-lak) as Principal.

6.   The Chimney was Warm

Kyung Hee Lee (이경희)

When I think of the Korean War, the first thing that comes to mind is the white porcelain sugar bowl in my friend Jonghui's house, which was in front of my house. Every day, we played together. Whenever I went to Jonghui's, her mom would scoop sugar from the bowl and make me sugared water in a large bowl. It was so refreshing and delicious!

One day, I went outside to play with Jonghui as usual, but I saw that many strange young men were moving all the furniture out of Jonghui's house. It looked as if the family was moving out. The one that caught my eyes was a man who was carrying the white porcelain sugar bowl. They all seemed thieves to me. I hurriedly ran back to my mom and said, "Mom, there are thieves at Jonghui's house; they're taking everything away." My mom held me tight and told me not to leave the house. The horrifying scene was deeply engraved in my head. Jonghui's father was a policeman. After that day, I never saw Jonghui and her family again. Her house remained empty.

Every time the siren rang, my family ran into the underground shelter. We had to stay quiet in the dark. I had to cover the mouth of my baby sister who was only two years old, when she started to cry. One day, my dad took my older sister on a bike to our maternal grandmother's. The next day, my mom took me to my paternal grandmother's house in Gimpo. Only my baby sister stayed with my parents. My parents thought it would be safer for me and my older sister to stay with our grand parents who lived in the countryside.

When we arrived at grandmother's house, mom left me after exchanging a few words with grandmother. When I followed my mom, I heard someone loudly singing a song of "The Moonlit Night of Shilla." Being left among the street peddlers, I cried and tried to run after her. But my mother did not look back and someone held me so tight that I couldn't move. Everyday I waited for her and ever since then the song"The Moonlit Night in Shilla" reminded me of the moment when my mom left me. And this is why I still stay away from listening to this song.

My grandmother's home was near the Gimpo airfields where the American soldiers stationed. And this place became my playground. When some soldiers waved at me, I went to them and sang for them. They gave me some chocolate and snacks.

When Gimpo became no longer a safe place from the war, we had to move into my great-aunt's home in Tongjin. It was a hot summer day when we set forth toward Tongjin on foot. It was very painful to walk on the sandy road for several hours. And whenever we heard the sound of the airplanes approaching, we threw ourselves on the sandy road.

At my great aunt's home, I was surrounded with nothing   familiar. I was uncomfortable and lonely and missed my parents. Especially during Chuseok (Korean Thanksgiving day), I was the only one, a refugee kid, who was wearing short sleeved summer chothes while other children were dressed in colorful Chuseok clothes. It was a chilly autumn day. The only warm place was the chimney outside the house. I sat down next to the warm chimney and cried.

Soon after chuseok, I moved back to my grandmother's house in Gimpo, where I felt at home. One day, my grandmother received a letter and after she read it, she began to pack and clean up the house. I remember that I had bothered her with questioning where we were going and whether I could meet my parents. Grandparents dug up the ground and buried some expensive items like silver spoons. They loaded straw bags of rice onto a pull cart, put me on the top and placed a bag of boiled chestnuts in front of me. All the adults walked the whole day heading for Incheon. I was reunited with my parents and my sisters there.

The next day, my family started our journey to the

south on a big ship. To get to the big transport ship, which was far off the shore, we stepped onto a small boat and then jumped onto another one and so on. The adults held my hands tightly so that I would not fall into the sea.

It makes me feel scary whenever I recollect this scene. Later in my high school senior year, passing a physical test became an entrance requirement for college. The long jump was especially terrifying for me, but the memory of jumping between small boats helped me practice repeatedly and overcome the dread of the long jump. Remembering that with a misstep I could fall into the sea, I did my utmost and was able to pass the exam.

In the cabin beneath the deck, we put the rice bags around us as fences. Our family of more than ten people had to eat only rice with Kimchi stew.

While on the ship toward south, my duty was to wait in line to get a bucketful of water assigned to each family for the day. It was a very important job for me. I was wondering why we suffered from the shortage of water since there were waters all around us. With a bucketful of water the entire family took turns to wash face with a wet towel. Doing laundry was beyond our dream. This experience taught me a lesson; do not waste water.

When the ship stopped at Mokpo, peddlers came onto the deck to sell food and other necessary items. We bought fish to make fish stew. Because there was not enough drinking water, we used seawater instead. Alas, it turned out too bitter to eat. The dire reality dawned upon me as a child that people could die due to the lack of water.

Whenever I went to the deck, the adults would grab my legs to prevent me from falling over the guard rails. But, I enjoyed the clear, bright sky. I still vividly remember how beautiful the sky was. While I felt the beauty of the sky and the sea, the adults were busy getting rid of lice in their underwear.

When our ship reached Busan, it seemed like a year to me to get there. But it actually took two weeks. In Busan we settled at a room on the second floor of a restaurant in Jungang-dong. Here I learned that a 'sabun' in Busan dialect meant a soap. Regardless of the language barrier, our landlord was so kind and helpful for my family and I still cannot forget his hospitality.

One day, something like a miracle happened to us. My uncle who was requisitioned for the red army during the war had appeared out of the blue. I was playing outside home in Jungang-dong. My uncle spotted me and finally joined the family. I don't know how to express the joy and excitement of my grandmother to get her son back. In retrospect, I cannot fathom all those troubles my uncle would have undergone to return home. Our family has, at last, survived this war.

Kyung Hee Lee served as a music teacher for 30 years and as vice-principal of Moon-young Girls' Middle School before retirement.

7. Exceptionally Cold Winter

Young Hee Lim (임영희)

Even more than half a century later, the "6.25 war" is deeply engraved in my memory, however vague it may be. When people mention '6.25,' the first thing that comes to mind is the Incheon Landing Operation (the secret code was 'Operation Chromite') since Incheon was where I spent my childhood since birth.

My dad's family originally lived in Pyongyang. My grandfather had studied at the Mining Department of Kyungsung High School (predecessor of College of Engineering, Seoul National University) during the Japanese colonial years. Upon graduation, he worked in Pyeongan Province where there were quite a few gold mines. Many of my relatives also lived in Pyongyang, and I remember calling them "Pyongyang aunt" to tell them apart from my "Haeju aunt." My grandfather was not rich, but comfortable enough to send my dad and his seven siblings to schools in Seoul, and some even to study abroad in Japan.

Incheon was the place where they ended up settling. They came with the sweeping crowd that migrated south following the "8.15 Independence." They probably chose Incheon because of its proximity to

North Korea while waiting for the right time to return to their hometown in the North. Perhaps that was why many North Korean refugees settled in Incheon.

As soon as the war broke out, my family rushed to Gagunneo, a small village near Incheon. I remember crossing the tideland sitting on a sack of rice on my father's back. Since rice was essential for survival, we carried rice everywhere we moved. We moved again from Gagunneo to Guweori, where there was the family burial mountain on my mom's side. I also remember my dad and uncle hiding in the attic of the groundskeeper.

There was an extremely scary moment. One day, my family happened to come face to face with five or six North Korean soldiers. They were disguised as farmers but carried a submachine gun wrapped in white cotton cloth. Terrified, my tender heart pounded terribly. Fighter jets were flying low over us, and blasting gunfire was heard in the distance. The men dragged me into the middle of the field, most likely in an attempt to avert the bombers away from them. Fortunately, as soon as the jets disappeared, they went quickly on their way. I suppose my family could have been annihilated on that day. I still get goose bumps when I think about that incident.

On September 15, 1950 while we were still living in

Guweori, there was a historic Incheon landing operation. The city lay in ruins as gunfire continued day and night off the coast. Our house in downtown Incheon was also bombed. I can still picture both my mom and grandma crying on its ruins, gutted of everything that was precious. Having lost our home, we lived off of my dad's friend until we were forced out again on the road with the 'January 4th Retreat.'

That winter was exceptionally cold. The Incheon coastal pier was filled with lots of refugees seeking passage to Busan. We boarded a small ship called Aguri (a military tank landing ship), then were transferred in the sea to a large vessel. All sorts of baggage and all kinds of people were tangled up with each other. My mom felt so seasick that she stayed in a crouched position. My face felt frozen, the biting wind turning my cheeks red. I felt sorry for myself as I trembled in the freezing cold. I couldn't stop stamping my feet. My dad took off his woolen gloves and put them on my feet.

On arrival in Busan, we rented a room in a shack on the hillside near Yeongdo Bridge. The roof leaked. It was so tiny that three of us could barely sleep in it with all of our luggage. I remember how the local children of the hillside village would relentlessly tease me, which never failed to end in my tears. We often ate mackerel which was cheap then. One day, I suffered from hives due to food poisoning. Ever since then, I developed similar symptoms to even into adulthood. And even now, I don't crave mackerel.

As a child, I experienced the war at the feet of the adults. Still, the horrors of the war, either heard of or experienced, remain indelibly etched in my memory even as long as seven decades. Whenever I have a chance, I talk to my family about what I have experienced. To our children and granddaughter, who have never experienced a war, it may be regarded as the reminiscence of old folks, but I always conclude by asserting that tragedy like this should never be repeated...

Dr. **Young Hee Lim** is a former professor of Food and Nutrition, Daejeon University. She taught Food and Nutrition for 37 years.

8.   What the War Brought Into My Life

Kyung-ja Uhm (엄경자)

As soon as we heard the first bomb explosion, my family fled the city of Chuncheon. Neither my three brothers nor I knew what was happening. We were frightened and confused. I still clearly remember my mom's frantic voice that we had to leave the city right away. A truck was parked in the center of the village, and we were told to get on it. I swiftly ran into the house, grabbed my school bag and a pair of sneakers that I had been saving for school, and climbed onto the truck. The truck took us to the edge of the Yangjoo River, where a large number of people had been waiting for boats, shouting and screaming. Finally, a boat arrived, and everyone clamored aboard. I barely made it on, pushed and shoved by the hysterical people. Once on the boat, all of us stayed upright, packed in a small space just like bean sprouts in a growing pot.

A few minutes into the river, the boat capsized. I found myself submerged in the river. I remember thinking, "I am going to die, and I won't be able to see my mom and family any more." Then suddenly a strong force lifted me and dumped me onto the sandy banks of the river.

Once on the south side of the river, we started our long walk to the south towards Busan. At one point, we came across a railroad bridge over a river, and somehow we needed to get to the other side. No one could explain how I did it, but I managed to pick my way atop the rickety tracks over the flowing water. I still shudder at the mere thought of it.

One day, we fortunately got a chance to ride a train, but only on its roof because the coaches were completely filled with refugees and their sacks filled with their belongings. All of a sudden, someone pushed my head down and whispered, "Be still!" The train moved into the darkness of a tunnel.

Smoke from the burning charcoal of the locomotive hit us hard. We felt choked to death while holding our breath. But as the train pulled out of the tunnel, the kids burst out laughing, pointing at each other. Everyone came out blackened with soot. All this still remains vivid in my memory.

When we arrived in Chungjoo we heard from someone that he had seen my dad. My dad had been in Seoul when the war broke out. If caught by the communists, he would have been killed because of his business involvement with the Korean government. So he was forced to leave immediately and run towards the south. At the news that my dad was alive, we were determined to find him, and our intensive search caught up with him in Daegu. He told us how he had managed to escape from Seoul. When my dad reached the bridge over the Han river, the bridge had already been bombed. He jumped into the river right away and crossed it, swimming and clinging to a piece of floating wood.

In Busan, we lived in a big complex building. Whenever I got bored, I taught myself the Korean alphabet while lying down on my tummy, using my older brother's textbooks. I also memorized multiplication tables that way.

After staying in Busan for a time, we were finally able to return to our beloved home, #95 Joongang-ro 1-ga, Chuncheon-si, Gangwon-do! I ran into the house, longing to see familiar things. To my disappointment, however, nothing remained the same. The air was stuffy and cold. The rooms were empty and turned upside-down. It was especially sad that the corn plants, which we had planted along the rear fence of the house, were no longer there.

My dad had his company building facing the main street, and our family quarters were in the back against the Bong-ye Mountain. We learned that the North Korean soldiers had used the company building as well as our house.

My brothers went out to look for Jjong, our family dog and a well-trained German Shepherd. When we were leaving Chuncheon in a hurry, Jjong followed us. But my mom shouted at Jjong, "Go back home!" At this he turned back and disappeared. He didn't look back, not even once. The villagers told us that the North Korean soldiers took him around wherever they went. On their retreat from the South, Jjong must have followed them. Poor Jjong! My brothers loved Jjong much more than I did.

When I returned home, I also learned that my best friend Songja had died. This meant the end of my childhood. The loss of Songja left me with an immense emptiness. Afterwards, as I was growing up, I often suffered from nightmares. In my dreams, I used to run through a tunnel, and crawl in the dark toward a light, which endlessly flickered on and off like a little dot! I would wake up startled in the middle of the night, drenched in sweat.

Recently, I decided to visit Chuncheon in search of the traces of my past, especially my beloved house. I was able to locate the exact spot where my family used to live. Now there stood a government building of Kangwon-do Province.

I am now retired and live in Canada, where I came as

a student more than 50 years ago. Reflecting on my childhood and the times since, I realize how deeply in love I am with my homeland, Korea. I know my love for her will stay strong for the rest of my life, and so will my hope and prayer for her.

Kyung-ja Uhm is a licensed pharmacist in Canada. Worked as a clinical pharmacist in the Ottawa Hospital at Civic Campus for 30 years before retirement.

9. The Story of My Bolero

Jean Yu (전정자)

When I read the book 'When Hitler Stole Pink Rabbit,' by Judith Kerr, a while back, my childhood memories came alive. 'Pink rabbit' was the author's beloved birthday present that she had left behind in Berlin home. It was a gray skirt that I had left behind in my room when my family rushed to escape from the war zone.

On an early morning in June in 1950, when the war broke out, my family left the home in a hurry. The next thing I can remember is being on the train heading south. When the train stopped for a short time around Daegu, my elder sister went out to get some hot water in our Thermos. We had a tall Thermos, something precious at the time. On her way back onto the train, she fell, and the glass-lined inside of the Thermos was broken into pieces. We all were so sad.

Right before the war, my mom got my elder sister and me new outfits of colorful flower embroidered gray skirts and matching boleros. That was the first nice thing I ever had. Beautiful thick silk flowers on gray fabric looked so elegant. Even though my father was a high-ranking government official before the war, I don't remember ever getting new clothes. I always got the hand-me-downs that became too small for elder sisters. I also don't remember the occasion why we got the new outfits, or whether all the kids in the family also got new clothes. I just remember my elder sister and I got the same new clothes.

Hurriedly leaving our home that morning, I forgot to bring that beautiful gray skirt. It was just my bolero that I had with me. For many days and months I regretted so much that I brought my bolero instead of the skirt. A skirt I could wear with other tops but the bolero alone was totally useless! Also, the bolero reminded me so much of the skirt I left behind. More, whenever I saw the bolero, it reminded me of our nice home in Seoul.

In Busan my family moved around a lot, staying in an old empty barracks, moving in with relatives, then to a large rental room, and so on. We didn't have much with us. We didn't need much either. In the summer, since our place was close to the beach we spent all the time at the beach.

When I came back to Seoul three years later, our home looked so different. The big yard and trees were still there, but somehow everything looked empty. The whole place seemed empty and deserted. There were huge white X marks taped on every window. That looked strange. I heard the North Korean Army used our house as their office building. They taped white papers on the windows, so no one could see inside.

People who left Seoul during the war were coming back every day. While waiting to go back to school, my sisters and I played in our big yard all day long.

One day we saw a few people moving about over the back fence, next to a narrow unpaved road. With the shovels they were carrying, they were digging in the ground right next to our fence. They were measuring the distance with their feet, marking a spot, and then digging and shoveling again. I didn't know what they were doing until they started weeping uncontrollably. Apparently, they must have buried their loved one there during the war, and now they are back to claim the remains. I remember one woman searching for the particular bowl she had buried near our house. I learned that when her husband died, she buried his body there and put a bowl next to his head. When she recognized the bowl, she fell over and wept. The sight haunts me even now.

Jean Yu wrote columns for Korean Daily Newspaper in Los Angeles, and also published a newsletter for Korean American Women.

Part 2. 70-Years Since

Our childhood experiences of the war are shared experiences. Every family was poor. It was of utmost importance to simply survive. Especially for children, to survive meant to be protected by the adults in the family.

It's been 70-years since the war. It took our classmates all over the world into various places and into all walks of life. And the stories are still unfolding.

10. A Little Girl on an Endless Road

Haerim Choi (최해림)

My first memory of the Korean War began at the Chungpa Community Center, Seoul. My mother must have had some errands to run there. When we left our home, we had no idea what laid ahead of us. All of sudden we heard a big explosion that shook the building and shattered the glass windows.

Mom instinctively covered me with her own body and crawled along the floor holding on to the legs of a table. After a while, things had calmed down. We got up and began to walk toward our home. Oh, I saw a bunch of people coming from the other side of the main street! They looked like a march of white ghosts! People were covered in ashes, bleeding and screaming. Mom covered my eyes so that I wouldn't see the scene of horror. But I saw everything and the scene was forever engraved in my memory! Later I learned that was the first bombing of Seoul on June 27, 1950, just 3 km away from where we were.

After that day, people were whispering words like 'reds,' 'women's alliance,' 'communists,' which I never heard of before. I was told my nickname was 'leech' in those days. My sister and brothers made fun of me saying, "When you were a little girl, you always clung to Mother's neck and did not leave her alone. She even had a hard time going to the bathroom." I don't have any memory of it, but I guess that poor little girl must have done so.

The next thing I remember is the day of our evacuation from Seoul to Busan in January, 1951. It was a dark winter morning. Our neighbor Mr. Gong kindly brought a cart and helped us load it with our belongings. There was a little space like a hole in the middle of the pile of boxes. Since I was the youngest, I was supposed to stay hunkered down there all the way to Incheon Harbor where we were supposed to catch a naval ship. We were to take refuge in Busan. We wore layers of clothing because not only was it cold, but also we had to take as much of our clothing as possible. I was there alone all day, surrounded by boxes in the middle of the cart. The Han River Bridge was already destroyed and we had to cross the river by a raft. My brother and I played with the water and were scolded because it was very dangerous and we could have drowned by accident.

It took a whole day to get to Incheon Harbor. It was already dark when we arrived there. My father and brother pushed the cart, while Mom and my sister walked on foot, following the cart but usually far behind. I tried hard to catch a glimpse of my mom and sister. Three families shared one room in a shabby house that night. I vaguely remember my brother crying that night and Father saying "Poor boy, you must be very tired. You were so courageous to push the cart whole day without complaining." Next day we took a small boat to get on the naval ship in the middle of the ocean. To get on board we had to climb a long ladder which didn't have any railing. We heard a big splash followed by screaming "someone fell off and drowned!" My mother kept saying "Hold tight! Don't let it go!" My parents were relieved when we all got on board safely. When I had a chance to talk about the refugee experience, my friends often said "That's nothing compared with what we had to go through! You really had it easy!"

I often had a nightmare during elementary school and once in a while in later years. The nightmare was related to the war -- I would be chased down by the communists. I would run and hide myself in a bunker. I would wake up terrified. When I returned to Korea from the United States in 1981 after my graduate studies in counseling psychology, I began to have this nightmare again. I had a difficult time readjusting to life in Korea. At that time, Korea was in a social turmoil which seemed to have brought back my anxiety.

One of the training components to become a therapist is the analysis of the self. One day when I was under analysis, I became aware of a little girl who was always following me. Was it a dream from my past or my imagination? She was a 6 or 7 year old girl and walking on an endless asphalt road under a blazing sun. There were no trees or grass along the road. It was so desolate. She was sweating and thirsty and almost in tears, wondering when this road was going to end.

I continued my free association which led to the forgotten little girl sitting in the refugee cart. The work of analysis slowly brought back my emotions -- how lonely and fearful I was on that cart. It is strange that I felt as if there were no other refugees on the road. All I remember was only our cart on the road. I was all alone the whole day in a tiny hole, surrounded by boxes. I was so alone. I was terrified. I didn't know how to articulate the feelings at the time, but I guess I was afraid of getting lost and becoming an orphan. That was why I tried so eagerly to catch the sight of my mother and sister. When they were out of my sight, I really wanted to cry out for them. But something made me hold back.

So I swallowed my tears. Even though it was winter, the sun at noon was warm and I wore layers of clothing which made me feel hot and sweaty. Obviously it was January, but my memory was distorted by how I felt. The little girl who followed me all the time was walking in the hot summer. But the feelings of loneliness, fear, and the urge to cry were the same. I knew I should control myself, endure, and not be a crying baby.

The fear since the bombing, together with the refugee experience in the cart somehow slipped away from my conscious life. It hid deeply in my unconscious world, but was still causing anxiety. I talked about the refugee experience, but didn't quite remember the emotion until the analysis. Once I was able to articulate my emotion, I finally realized who the little girl was. After the emotions of the little girl were deeply appreciated and accepted with empathy, the girl did not appear anymore. I no longer had the nightmare. I was free from her!

The experience could have been just one of those experiences anyone could have had during a war. But to young children, it could become a trauma that remains throughout their lives. Traumas such as physical destruction, social turmoil, economic loss, separation of families, and death are often discussed as war damages. How about the pains that each person experienced? We experienced the Korean War 70 years ago, but the essays of our classmates tell us they carry the pains in their hearts so vividly even now! You see the same in Secondhand Time Hand: The Last of the Soviets by Svetlana Alexievich, 2015 Noble Prize in Literature. My heart cries out for those children living in war every day somewhere in this world. No wars on this earth! No more wars!

Indulging in my reminiscence, I still remember the light breath of my mother who threw herself to protect me. I miss her and her love.

Haerim Choi is a private practice counselor, a former professor of psychology, Sogang University, Seoul, and former President of Korean Counseling and Psychotherapy Association.

11. Crown and Mask

Jung-im Yum (염정임)

As masked people holding umbrellas approach in the city rain, their expressionless faces look as strange as Rene Magritte's paintings.

The life we have been living lately is like an artificial reality. Each morning the news announces the number of newly infected people like a weather forecast. Every day is like a futuristic science fiction movie, where there is a battle waging between the crown and the mask.

Wearing its crown, the invisible virus attacks humankind, and all humans are defending themselves by wearing masks. Right now, the crown possesses an absolute advantage. First off, the crowns are invisible, so the masks as a visible defense seem to be at a distinct disadvantage.

Masks hide people's personalities, as well as their character and dignity. But in a way, humans already live everyday wearing their masks. Behind the mask, we don't know what someone thinks or who they are. Even greed and hate can be hidden behind a mask.

With their masks on, it could be that humans may become more homogenous and believe that there's only one way to see others: me versus my enemies.

The crown was always necessary to show the king's authority. Human history is a history of warring over the crown. It's very symbolic that the virus has the shape of a crown. It understands human nature so well.

Just as the emperor ruled with absolute power, the crown has always ruled over the mask. Wearing their crowns, the kings in the past were always entertained by their masked jesters.

Today, the virus might be laughing as it watches people armed with their masks.

Our emotions fluctuate daily as the numbers go up and down, and the crown is laughing.

Every opportunity it gets, the crown accumulates power to destroy humanity. In the 14th century, it used rats as the host to spread the virus. Now, many centuries later it laughs at the power-hungry human race as it attacks humans in the shape of a crown.

The virus craftily isolates people from churches and from society. The people who were gathering and dreaming about peace in heaven have grown accustomed to worshipping through their smartphones like some sort of shadow worship.

A Greek philosopher once said this world is the shadow of the heavens. Humans are captivated by the shadows in a huge cave, thinking the shadows are reality.

Every day these nervous and incomplete creatures live with hope in one moment and hopelessness in the next. There must be some secret behind these infection numbers. Maybe it is sending us a code?

In some countries, there are just too many dead bodies to bury properly. Human dignity is being destroyed in a devastating manner, and the global clock has been turned back to the 14th century, when the pest was thriving. All the cultural, scientific, medical, and technological advancements are becoming ineffective in this battle.

As the crown mutates, its ability to infect gets stronger. Just as the masks that actors wear in Peking Operas continuously change, so too should we change our masks every hour?

Maybe looking at the virus and humans from a distant universe would show they are all mere specks.

Who will win between the crown and the mask?

Perhaps this universe is the creator's big chess board.

Whose hand will the creator raise to declare the victor?

Jung-im Yum is a debut Essayist and a winner of many literary awards, including Hyundai Best Literary Essay Award of 2020.

12. Grandpa's Inheritance

Jungsoon Ryu (유정순)

We are a refugee family from Pyongyang, North Korea. Since the Japan-Korea Annexation Treaty of 1910, Korea was deprived of her administration of internal affairs along with her diplomatic rights. Independence activists rose up in resistance against Japan, like the March 1st Movement of 1919. The spirit spread throughout the whole nation with resistance movements at home and abroad, leading to the establishment of a Provisional government in Shanghai in April 1919.

You are a granddaughter of a martyr.

One thing I and my older siblings often heard growing up was that we were descendants of a martyr.

There are countless stories of unsung heroes, including the sacrifices of people of faith who stood against the brutal rule of Japan. The events of my grandfather's life, and the conflicts that he personally engaged in the fight for independence, were more dramatic and frightening than any movie thriller I have ever seen.

The outlook was bleak for Korea as suppressed people rapidly lost any hope for survival. At the same time, Western missionaries were becoming a familiar sight on the streets of Pyongyang. Grandpa initially numbered among those who regarded them as foreign intruders to be driven out from our territory. One day, he confronted one of 'the peddlers of foreign religion,' named Samuel Moffet, and physically knocked him down.

This inauspicious beginning developed into a friendship that changed the destiny of my grandpa and his descendants. The day grandpa accepted to trust in the name of Jesus, he severed the topknot on his head as a symbol of a fresh beginning of new life. He then gave Moffet free use of the guest quarter of his house for teaching the Bible to other Koreans.

Grandpa's business involved importing and exporting salt and coal between China and Korea. He owned over ten ships and even more boats used to transport cargo in and out of Pyongyang. His warehouse by the Daedong River was always bustling with traders, businessmen and laborers.

This business provided the perfect shield for grandpa's secret role as Regional Director of the Shanghai Provisional Government of Korea. His resistance work was multi-faceted. He harbored independence fighters and arranged for their safe exit from the country. He also transported and distributed newspapers for the resistance published at headquarters in Shanghai. And he raised funds for the provisional government and sent it safely to Shanghai.

Unexpected torrential rain was particularly dangerous. My grandpa would have to move masses of straw sacks of salt, and the newspapers they concealed, to avoid being washed out, but even more desperately to avoid detection by the Japanese authorities.

Grandpa was an elder of Sanjunghyun Church in Pyongyang where Pastor Joo Ki-chul served. He was greatly impressed by Pastor Joo who had preached against the Shinto worship coerced by Japanese authority. Joo was imprisoned, brutally tortured and finally died during his imprisonment.

Japan surrendered in 1945. The excitement of independence lasted only a few days as Russian soldiers soon marched into Pyongyang. Their barbaric behavior and violence caused people to flee south resulting in Korea's national migration. Grandpa urged grandma and all of his family to leave quickly, assuring them that he would follow soon but knowing that he would never do so.

In May 1950, the Communist Party of North Korea forcibly assumed control of the Sanjunghyun church, which was the birth place of martyrdom and the base of Korean nationalism. Grandpa's house became the secret place of worship in its stead. On June 24, 1950, grandpa was arrested and taken away by the State Political Security Department (SPSD) of North Korea. And on October 18, 1950, he was shot on the banks of his beloved Daedong River. Eyewitnesses of the execution reported this later as the SPSD must have decided to dispose of its prisoners on the eve of their retreat. The Allied Forces recaptured the city of Pyongyang on October 19,1950 according to official documents.

You are an Ambassador of Korea.

I went to America to study as soon as I graduated from Ewha University. On my departure, my father told me not to forget my roots and remember that, wherever I went in America, I went as 'an ambassador of Korea.' He urged me to be careful to not shame my country while living abroad.

I was deeply moved by the example of my mother when she had attended Donjisa University in Japan during the colonial years. She had served in her Korean church there every Sunday by playing the organ. And she had chosen always to wear to church a hanbok (Korean traditional dress) with a black skirt and a white top. On her walk to church, she endured all kinds of ridicule; even small Japanese children would throw stones at her.

My parents were amazing patriots. On their wedding night in occupied Pyongyang, they softly sang all four stanzas of the Korean national anthem following prayers for the country. I still do not know all the lyrics of the national anthem myself.

We see that difficult times produce exceptional heroes out of ordinary people.

The generations before us gallantly fought the fight for independence. That knowledge was how I preserved my Korean identity even as I lived in the United States of America as a citizen for many decades.

I married a surgical resident who had come to America two years before me. On the weekends we often opened our apartment to homesick, Korean students to enjoy each other's company over a simple meal and vent our pent-up emotions. In the late 1960s most Korean students depended largely on scholarships, for the Korean government forbade any international transaction of currency. Therefore, we shared our desperate thirst for good grades and English language competency in order to succeed in our academic programs.

Bound by a common destiny, we experienced a

strong sense of community. It became a tradition that, when anyone moved to another university in a different state, the student would sell his furniture and kitchen supplies to a new student at a fraction of the cost.

In the meantime, the gathering of students and medical residents naturally developed into a Korean church. And a few years later, we started a Korean language school that met on Saturdays. This was before the Korean government supported Korean schools abroad. We, parents of the same vision, made textbooks ourselves using steel pens and mimeograph machine. It was analog publishing. My husband composed the school song, and my father wrote the lyrics. Our little Korean school began with singing the Korean National Anthem followed by the Korean school song. Children were also taught music, Korean traditional dance and taekwondo.

The city where we lived held an annual International Festival in the Civic Center. Our Korean school proudly represented Korea there. Our Korean dance team and taekwondo team became the highlights of the festival.

Invest in people.

My father practiced medicine until he was in his late 80s. His discipline of regular exercise and self-fulfillment in work kept his life satisfying. My mother, on the other hand, served 'the least of these,' helping regularly for over 45 years at an orphanage, a home for unwed mothers, a Navy detention center, the VA hospital, and so on. Whenever anyone from any of these facilities needed medical care, my father saw them for free.

One day a girl from the orphanage came running and crying to my mother. She escaped with her life, running barefoot on concrete for thirty minutes until she reached my parents' house. My mom took her in and cared for her. When it was time for her to marry, she chose instead to live with my parents and help them with their household and medical practice. She lived with them for 37 years. When my parents passed away, my siblings and I counted her as one of us and executed the will accordingly.

We have seen my parents repeatedly grieved by misplaced trust in people. Yet we have seen them turn around and extend their hand to help out over and over again. They taught the incomparable value of people over money. When I received my portion of the family inheritance, I wanted to honor their legacy by using the money to imitate their life example.

At the time, my husband and I supported a Korean missionary to India. She taught children who came from extreme poverty and couldn't afford an education.

She gathered them in a makeshift hut constructed of straw and branches to shade them from the scorching heat of the sun. But whenever there was a downpour of rain, the school hut was swiftly swept away, and the children were forced into a long vacation.

As soon as monsoon season was over, the children and the missionary would start to gather branches and straw to build the school hut all over again.

I remembered that my grandpa had also served for many years as chairman of the Soongduk School Foundation, which helped to produce a great number of youth leaders for Korea. With that in mind, it was natural to choose to help build a school in my parents' honor. Today, the red brick school building stands tall in Santiniketan,

India, welcoming many children even in monsoon season.

Seek after things of eternal value.

When I was younger, I assumed that the first fruit of martyrdom in my family was my grandpa in North Korea. But unexpectedly, a new piece of documentation was delivered to us, and I was speechless.

- Ryu, Jingil (Agustino), 49 yrs. Martyred in 1839. Crackdown by King Heonjong.
- Ryu, Daechul (Peter), 13 yrs. Son of Ryu Jingil.

Martyred in 1839.

- Ryu, Jungyul (Peter), 30 yrs. Martyred in 1866. Crackdown by King Gojong.

In celebration of the 200th anniversary of the Catholic Church of Korea, Pope John Paul II visited Korea. The highlight of his visit was the canonization ceremony for the 103 Korean martyrs on May 6, 1984. My forefathers were among them.

There is yet another surprise. It was a gift from above. Grandpa had three men who shared a sense of kinship with him in carrying out the clandestine activities in support of the Provisional Government of Shanghai. One of them was a fellow member of the church and was solely responsible for collecting funds for the resistance and channeling it safely to Shanghai. He was unfortunately apprehended and tortured with the goal of revealing the list of contributors and his compatriots. He remained silent. He was imprisoned and later released only to die at home. This man's great-grandson is my son-in-law. I found it out some decades later.

My second daughter and my son-in-law graduated from elite universities on the east coast. They were quite accomplished scholars with two master's degrees each. However, they chose to live with those who needed not only their knowledge but also their hearts. They have been multiplying blessings since.

The path my grandpa had walked on, assigning value to eternal things, is one I want to follow for the rest of my life. And I want to pass this vision down to the next generation.

Jungsoon Ryu studied at Case Western University, and Liberty U. Worked as a family counselor in Ohio, USA, and Korea.

13. A Tribute to My Mother

Yoon-kyung Lee (이윤경)

About 70 years ago, during the Korean War, I was once separated from my family while we fled Seoul on foot. My parents had their hands full with my two baby sisters and heavy bags of survival essentials, so I must have been walking on my own. I dimly recall being part of a large crowd of refugees, all of us trying to get to a place of greater safety. A single moment of distraction was all it took, and I was carried off into the crowd.

I don't remember much of what happened, other than it was evening when my mother found me, wandering lost down a street of some homes. But one memory shines more clearly - when my mother found me, she asked: "where is your other shoe?" I must have lost one shoe somewhere.

I regret that I never asked my mother how she had found me. I could have asked her so many things. I could have acknowledged all the sewing she had done during the war to feed a large family (there were more than ten of us, including several distant relatives). I could have asked her how it was like to be a woman raising and educating four children alone after my father passed away. Most of all, I could have thanked her for finding me.

Despite my many regrets, I must have given her some joys. Especially during her final years, she couldn't get enough of my stories - stories about my colleagues, even about the papers I wrote and talks I gave at conferences. She revelled in hearing about my professional 'successes', in particular, no matter how small or mundane. The following is a tribute to my mother in heaven.

I devoted almost my entire career to computer science research at the IBM T. J. Watson Research Center. Artificial Intelligence (AI) and its related areas were always at the forefront of my research interests.

Currently, the term AI is commonplace in everyday life - we don't need to browse Netflix for very long before finding a plethora of movies featuring self-aware and intelligent machines. But in the real world, too, AI is known. In 2016, major television networks throughout Korea broadcasted the defeat of Go master Lee Se-dol by AlphaGo, an AI-enabled computer Go program. That wasn't the first time a computer defeated a human, of course. Computer programs have been able to defeat the best human chess players ever since 1997 when IBM's Deep Blue supercomputer won against chess champion Gary

Kasparov.

But back when I started my career, .. it wasn't easy to explain to a non-professional in simple terms what specific research issues I was working on. Back then, most people had not even heard of the term AI before and talking about what I did professionally was a guaranteed way to kill a conversation.

After AlphaGo, people's awareness of AI (and of the Fourth Industrial Revolution) has become heightened, and I have had some opportunities to give lectures on the subject.

Perhaps surprisingly, religious sisters of the Roman Catholic Church are especially interested in learning about AI. Their pastoral duties often involve caring for a generation of people who have diverse interests, including AI, Machine Learning, and the extent to which the latest scientific discoveries and developments can potentially affect our religious belief.

As I start venturing into the possibilities of AI, there is an anchor point that I try not to forget, something that even the latest technological advancements have yet to overcome: it is easy to teach a computer the professional knowledge and analytic skills an adult can acquire. But it is not easy at all to understand how a 3-year old child can learn so much, so quickly.

Alan Turing, widely considered to be the father of modern computer science, said that the gist of AI is not in building a machine that replicates an adult human's cognitive ability; it is, instead, to build a 'child machine' that behaves just like a child. Turing's pioneering claim was that for a machine to be considered intelligent it should behave and think like a child. Can someone design an intelligent machine before the end of the 21st century that can pass the Turing test? We don't know.

Although it falls far short of passing the Turing test, AI technologies in the 21st century have achieved dramatic accomplishments. It is especially so in the areas of speech and natural language recognition, machine learning, and complex data analytics.

On the other hand, there are quite a few people who are concerned that the new technologies could be abused for destructive purposes. They point out that now we can reengineer even the human brain and the mind, but what we know about their destructive possibilities is very limited.

How, then, can we respond to the destructive potential? How can we make wise choices for both the present and the future of humanity?

That's a serious and important conversation to engage in. But at this current moment in time, my attention is focused on an immediate need - exploring tangible ways in which AI can help with the coronavirus pandemic.

AI robots are becoming more common in healthcare settings from sanitizing hospital rooms to delivering supplies, and identifying a patient with a fever. The most urgent topic during the coronavirus pandemic is, however, that of developing an effective vaccine and/or finding treatment drugs for coronavirus. Challenges in this task are many. For one, vaccine development or drug discovery in general is a lengthy, expensive process. Moreover, scientists point out that the speed at which the coronavirus mutates, with new variants emerging continuously, may out speed the vaccine/ drug development process.

There are certain AI methodologies that can help scientists shorten the time it takes for the process. AI can analyze large and complex data at a speed that traditional methods won't be able to match.

For those who have been wondering why it's such a big deal for the program AlphaGo to master Go, especially compared to earlier successes, notably with Chess, the explanation is this: the number of possible Go games is almost endless. As some say, "the search space in Go is vast... the number greater than there are atoms in the universe." Instead of searching all potential moves, AlphaGo was trained to learn new strategies by itself and could frequently predict the next human moves without searching through all the potential moves—which is impossible to do in a limited time.

In the search for coronavirus drugs, currently, one of the most promising approaches is that of repurposing existing drugs, which have already been approved for different diseases. There are about 4,000 approved drugs on the market today.

But analyzing all of the 4,000 drugs is far from being enough. Their combinations should be considered. Scientists say that it is unlikely that one single drug would be the answer for coronavirus. To show how much time the process would take, here is an example.

Given 4,000 existing drugs, the total number of 2- or 3-drug combinations that are to be analyzed can be:

- 2-drug pairs: 8 million possible pairs
- 3-drug triples: 10.5 billion triples.

It will take a traditional method too much time for it to be useful, while AI technology can dramatically speed up the initial work of searching through the possible combinations of possible ingredients such as above. This is the reason why AI is seen as one of the essential tools that is available to humans for taming the coronavirus.

AI may have been overhyped or subject to larger ethical concerns. Nevertheless, it is our responsibility to understand the new technologies and find a balance between the benefits and the risks. To achieve this balance, we cannot afford to ignore uncomfortable changes the new technologies may bring. Rather, we need to understand the impacts the changes may have on our daily lives.

Would my mother have understood this? I say "Yes."

Dr. Yoon-kyung Lee is a former Research Scientist at the IBM T. J. Watson Research Center, NY.

14. The Image of Sunrise

Jung-yoon Lee (이정윤)

Translated by Yoonyoung Kim (김윤영)

The sun comes up every day. It never fails to rise, but each day with a unique aura and hue. Every sunrise is a mystic experience for me. The way I appreciate watching a sunrise has changed as time has gone by. In my youth, I was overwhelmed with excitement for no reason when I saw the soaring sun conquer the darkness. But now I feel overcome with reverence and humility. Thrilling splashes have become tranquil, yet trailing gentle waves.

Putting my hands together, I lower my head in prayer, first for my family and then my country. Sometimes my prayer extends out to all living things in the world.

There is the Gold Coast, 40km in length along the east coast of Australia. The long stretch of fine sand turns glorious golden at sunrise and sunset. The season there is opposite to the one in Korea, the Jacaranda trees lined along the boulevards usher in spring with magnificent clouds of purple blooms in September.

I arranged a place to stay in the Gold Coast for my return trip close to the beach where I had often strolled along with my family when we had lived there. The back of the motel to the beach, it provided us with a great ocean view through the living room and bedroom. I made myself get up early every day to greet the sunrise during our stay.

One day I stepped out to the veranda with a shawl around me. It was around four o'clock in the morning. Sitting in the still darkness I, holding my breath, marveled at the layers of darkness peeling away. The sea and the sky became one, sinking in a shade of ash grey. I was gazing out over the dark sea ahead while listening to the ceaseless breakers surging upon the shore. As darkness pared away little by little, it turned pale grey, tinged with delicate purple, pastel pink, and then, blended orange. After the color of red spread slowly, the sky between the sea and the cloud began to be smeared with crimson, as the low-lying band of grey clouds gradually rose up the sky. Then the cloud band turned cream, pink, and scarlet, and the color of each layer of cloud changed in different shades little by little. The core, looking like a flaming wick, quivered at the moment, the horizon turned crimson, and the sun's red forehead suddenly emerged above the ocean. It seemed to take only two or three minutes to reveal its entire spherical appearance. Another reminder of how fast the earth turns.

What is this cosmic space where the sun, a blazing ball of fire, is floating, I wonder. I feel smaller than a speck of dust. Fingernail sized crabs hiding in tiny holes in sand, seagulls flying along the seashore searching for food at daybreak, and myself are all helpless small beings in mother nature.

Even though we live in an era when science is so advanced and the secrets of the universe are unveiled a layer at a time, the red sun soaring from total darkness remains a mystery and pulls me to yearn for something. I have come to understand why the sun was worshiped in ancient Egypt.

If a sunrise is merely a routine every day, I would not watch it with bated breath, with my heart fluttering at every daybreak. No matter how tough and stormy your life is, there is hidden hope and joy as the sun never fails to rise, even on rainy days, even when it is hiding above a thick layer of stormy clouds.

It is said that an African tribe gathers around to sing and stamp their feet to please the sun, fearing that it might not come up. The sun breathes in life and gives life to the whole universe. I, too, beat my spiritual drum today, calling my renewing sun to rise strong.

Jung-yoon Lee is Modern Essay Debut Essayist.
Yoonyoung Kim is a cellist, and Doctor of Muscal Arts.

Part 3. Special Contribution

As we capture the stories of our childhood war memories in writing, it seemed worthwhile to also provide a brief background on the state of the national defense at the time the war broke out. Thus, we carry here an excerpt from Gen. (ret) Chung Yul Kim's memoir, who was Chief of Staff of the Korean Air Force at the time.

Also, a special contribution is by Jean Lee, a former AP Seoul bureau chief who also opened the news agency's bureau in Pyougyang, North Korea. Her essay is based on the story of her own family, written from the viewpoint of a journalist.

The essay by H.J. Choi addresses a variety of 6.25-related topics embedded in the tragedies faced by the individual family members, such as left-right division, defection, carnage perpetrated on both sides, abduction of important figures, loss of Korean heritage.

15. Status of South Korean National Defense

At the Outbreak of the Korean War

Taeja Kim Lee (김태자)

Translated by Yer-ae K. Choi

<This article is based on Aviation Alarm, a memoir written by the author's father, Gen.(ret) Chung Yul Kim (Daehee Publishing, 2010).>

When the Korean War broke out, my father was Chief of Staff of the Korean Air Force. As the original founder of the Air Force, subsequently serving as the first and third Chief of Air Force and then the seventh Minister of National Defense, he played a central role in the development of South Korean national defense.

With the establishment of the South Korean government on August 15, 1948 and the appointment of Bum Seok Lee as Minister the following day, the Ministry of National Defense was launched. The Ministry of Defense had its origin in the Ministry of Communications, a division of the US Military Government. Its Chosun Guard became the Army and its Chosun Coast Guard, the Navy. The air force was a part of the Army, not an independent entity. The US Government deemed it highly unlikely that the Soviet Union, after the decisive assistance it received from the US during WWII, would provoke a new war. This optimistic outlook resulted in limiting Korea's defense to general public safety and neglecting to secure basic arms such as tanks and fighter aircrafts. North Korea, on the other hand, had been strengthening its army since 1946, and when it conducted its invasion into South Korea in 1950, owned 242 T-34 tanks and 226 fighter aircrafts.

Although the South Korean air force had an army air base command, it did not own one single aircraft. On September 4, 1948, it acquired ten L-4s from the US Army, and on September 15, with my father as formation leader, these aircrafts, painted with the *Taegeuk* symbol, flew the sky over Seoul for the first time in the nation's history. On December 23, the US Army, recognizing the capabilities of the Korean pilots, gave them ten L-5s, bringing the total number of the liaison aircrafts to 20. In January 1949, the Army Aviation Academy opened, and my father was appointed its first principal.

The Academy faced severe financial hardship, as illustrated by the events occurring at our house in Donam-dong. In the backyard stood a single medium-sized truck whose engine sputtered to life only after a big push by several men. No one knew how to drive the truck, so my father filled in as chauffer. Every day, morning and evening, he gave rides to his staff and instructors, picking them up and dropping them off at their houses scattered around Seoul. Due to a tight budget, the entire staff ate the meager meals issued by the military. Only the instructors were treated with *omurice* specially ordered from the local eateries.

My father spared no effort to make the air force independent. In April of 1949, he self-published a pamphlet titled 'Aviation Alarm,' in which he stressed the critical importance of independent air force given the confrontational situation with North Korea as well as the urgent need to secure fighter aircrafts. Even as the positive response from various sectors of society grew, the US Army decided, in June of 1949, to withdraw its troops. President Syngman Rhee took this opportunity to make a strong plea to US for additional aid. Mere $98,000, out of the total military aid of $11,300,000, had been allocated for aircraft fighters. The plea went unheard. In August of 1949, President Rhee, concluding that sole reliance on US aid was inadequate, launched a fundraising campaign, 'Pan-National Patriotic Campaign for Aircrafts.' The enthusiastic support of Koreans made it possible to soon meet its goal of $300,000.

With the success of the campaign, the air force finally gained its independence in October of 1949. At the age of 32, my father, Chung Yul Kim, Air Force dog tag No.1 50001, became Chief of General Staff of the Air Force. Every Saturday the airmen from all corners of the country met at our house in Donam-dong and organized a corps of 1,600 men. My grandmother, a woman of considerable means, provided food and lodging for the men who visited our house in Donam-dong to attend the meetings. According to Gen. (ret) Kim Doo-man, 'in a sense, the establishment of Korean Air Force was made possible by the generosity of the entire Kim family. We are truly grateful.'

Despite the success of the fundraising campaign, the actual purchase of the aircraft fighters met with hurdles. As the US policy prohibited the sale of fighter aircrafts, the only option was Canada's AT-6, single-engined advanced trainer aircrafts. Ten of these were purchased at $27,000 each, and the remaining $30,000 secured 1,000 drums of gasoline. The AT-6 aircrafts began to arrive in Korea on March 15, and on May 14 were named 'National Foundation Aircrafts.' This was 40 days prior to the breakout of the Korean War.

What was the status of the Army? The Navy? The Army consisted of 96,140 men and had no tank. North

Korea had 242 tanks. The Navy had 7,715 men and had security guard ships but no warship. This was the status of South Korean national defense on June 25, the day the country was attacked by the North.

In the predawn hours of June 27, the commanding officers of the Army, Navy, and Air Force met at the National Defense Headquarters in Yongsan to plan operations. At daybreak the Air Force, after burning important documents, began preparing for their retreat to Suwon. With only 17 vehicles available, they decided to take 500 combat-ready men, leaving behind the Women's Aviation Training Group and the Men's Training Group. 500 drums of gasoline and 23 trainer aircrafts would follow.

Early morning of June 26, President Rhee placed a call to General MacArthur requesting immediate assistance. General MacArthur, fully aware of South Korea's lack of fighter aircrafts, decided to send ten F-51Ds and dispatched ten pilots to Itazuke Air Base in Japan, a forward base in the Southwest region of the Far East US Air Force.

At 11:30 on June 28, the capital city of Seoul fell to the North Korean People's Army. The 10 South Korean pilots who arrived at Itazuke Air Base had only received land training due to bad weather, and on July 1, with barely 30 minutes of combat training under their belt, hurriedly returned to the battlefront. For several days, the field pilots did whatever they could in their flimsy liaison aircrafts, which lacked cabin covers and could only accommodate two men. The men in the back seat threw down bombs and grenades with their bare hands until, on July 3, the trained pilots from Japan arrived. Sadly, the flight commander Geon Seok Lee was killed on his first sortie. On July 5, 1950, President Rhee, in spite of an extremely dangerous environment, insisted on an aerial inspection of the frontline. According to the witness account of Gen. (ret) Yoon Eung-ryul, my father piloted T-6 carrying the president.

The South Korean pilots received regular training from the US pilots and conducted joint sorties. However, in an effort to hold down the number of casualties, the inadequately trained pilots numbering about 30 trained separately on their own. It was during one of these training missions that the operation to save the Tripitaka Koreana at Haeinsa Temple was successfully executed.

In the early hours of June 28, President Truman decided to send US troops to Korea and called a meeting of the United Nations Security Council to urge its member nations to send their troops as well. My father writes in his memoir, 'The US entry into the

Korean War was a miracle.' It is clear that if the UN forces had not entered the war, Korea as we know it would not have existed. The total number of soldiers the UN member nations sent to Korea was 1,651,849 (US 1,500,000). The total dead numbered 40,673 (US 39,940), and injured, 115,450 (US 103,284). The number of MIAs and POWs reached roughly 10,000.

Among the US generals who fought during the Korean War, 142 were joined by their sons. 35 of them gave their lives. General Walton H. Walker, who died during the war, fought with his son Captain Sam Walker (later rose to the rank of four-star general). James Van Fleet, son of General James Van Fleet, Jr., a fighter bomber pilot, perished near the Yalu River. President Eisenhower's son, John Eisenhower, fought in the war. Captain William Clark, son of Mark Clark (Commander of the United Nations Forces), died from complications of head injuries he sustained. Allen M. Dulles, son of Allen Dulles (Director of Central Intelligence Agency), was shot in the head and suffered life-long schizophrenia. (Kim Deok-soo, *Aviation Records*)

So many from the US and 16 other nations sacrificed their lives in defense of South Korea, a tiny country whose name might well have been unfamiliar to them. Here I am reminded of a passage from my father's memoir: "A sage of old once said, 'If one prays to a star with a grateful heart, the Goddess of Happiness will bestow moonlight. If one prays to the moonlight with a grateful heart, she will bestow bright sunlight.' Even during the time of great challenge, if we strive to lead righteous lives, our society will enjoy purity and beauty."

Taeja Kim Lee is a founding member of the Korea Music Foundation and Sejong Soloists in NY, and Music in PyeongChang in Korea. Also served as Advisory Board Chairperson of Korean American Community Foundation in NY.

16. Guns and Hunger

Jean H. Lee (이준희)

<This essay first appeared in the Summer 2020 issue of the Wilson Quarterly.>

On the morning of June 25, 1950, my father, the mischievous fourth son of a prosperous South Korean businessman, was fast asleep in the family's home in Gangwon Province. It was a quiet morning in an otherwise bustling home where his mother watched over four sons and two daughters, with another on the way. Her husband was in Seoul for work with their second son, then attending high school in the capital.

Times were tense. For months, skirmishes with North Korean soldiers had been taking place along the 38th Parallel, a stone's throw to the north, and South Korean troops were busy fending them off. Despite the constant threat of war, my father recalls an idyllic childhood in the big house in Chuncheon, swimming in the river in the summers and ice skating in the winters.

But in the predawn hours of June 25, North Korean troops massed along the border dividing North and South, and staged an invasion by land and air that stretched from west to east. Seoul, the South Korean capital, was their main target.

As North Korean soldiers closed in, my grandfather and his son jumped into a rented truck. They made it across the Han River before the bridge was bombed to slow the communist advance.

Meanwhile, in Chuncheon, my pregnant grandmother made a split-second decision to flee on foot with the children — including my father — and two household helpers.

For the next eight months, the family faced hunger and starvation as they crisscrossed the country dodging North Korean troops and bombings by the US-led United Nations forces. My grandmother lost one son and gave birth to a daughter. Three of my father's uncles went missing.

When the fighting came to a halt with an Armistice Agreement three years later, on my father's 13th birthday, July 27, 1953, the family returned to Seoul to rebuild their lives.

My family's wartime tale is not particularly remarkable; their harrowing experience could be told a million times over. This is not a tale of military heroism, or even one of selfless sacrifice. It is simply the story of one family of ordinary Koreans who survived the three cruel and crushing years of war that killed nearly a million South Korean civilians.

In looking back at the AP's wartime dispatches, I was dismayed to see the people of Korea referred to routinely as "peasants," a demeaning term that stripped them of identity and diminished the significance of their lives.

On this 70th anniversary, as we honor the veterans who fought on their behalf, I want to put names and faces to these "peasants," starting with my family.

The Fall of Seoul

Today, North Korea remains one of the world's poorest nations even as the regime has built one of most dangerous nuclear programs on the planet. South Korea, meanwhile, has risen in global stature to become the world's 12th-largest economy, and a leader in technology, healthcare and pop culture.

But in 1950, South Korea also was impoverished. It was struggling to transition to democracy after more than 35 years of colonial oppression by the Japanese and, before that, centuries of a feudal monarchy.

Five years earlier, after surrendering during World War II, Japan had finally withdrawn from South Korea. In its wake, the Soviet Union sent soldiers from the north while the United States brought in troops from the south, dividing Korea at the 38th Parallel.

The Soviets installed the young Kim Il Sung in

Pyongyang. In September 1948, he established the Democratic People's Republic of Korea and became its first leader. The United States backed the American-educated Syngman Rhee in Seoul, who was elected president of the new Republic of Korea. Both declared their administrations the legitimate government of Korea.

By early 1950, my paternal grandfather, Lee Pom-rae, owned a string of gasoline stations in Gangwon Province, in South Korea's northeast. Young, successful and well-connected, he also was politically active, funding the local office of the ruling party, supporting President Rhee and donating generously to the Red Cross. He also had political aspirations; he ran for a seat in the new National Assembly in March 1950 — and lost.

On June 25, he was in Seoul on business with son Hak-chong, who was attending school in the capital. As the North Korean troops advanced, my grandfather tried frantically to reach the family in Chuncheon. But the roads northeast were blocked, so they drove south.

"As we crossed [the] Han River and drove southward, the road became completely filled with evacuating traffic and refugees, making it impossible for a vehicle to drive on," Hak-chong, known to me and my cousins as Uncle Hank, recalled in a memoir written before his

2016 death. "No sooner (had) our truck slowed down than the refugees swarmed over and completely packed it. Refugees continued to pour into the road, and the traffic was virtually immobile."

It took hours to drive a few miles to Suwon, on the capital's southern outskirts. "Just before the daybreak, we heard a big, big blast from north." A South Korean military engineer had been ordered to blow up the Han River Bridge in a bid to stop the North Korean advance, killing hundreds of civilians and soldiers trying to flee south. "It meant the North Korean takeover of Seoul was imminent, if not already taken over."

Seoul fell to the North Koreans in just three days.

Giving up hope of reaching Chuncheon, my grandfather continued south to Yeongdong, his wife's hometown in North Chungcheong Province. There, my grandmother's family, the Songs, were landowners with a sprawling traditional Korean "hanok" estate. The Songs descended from an illustrious poet, philosopher and statesman, Song Si-yeol, and for hundreds of years had maintained a traditional Confucian lifestyle.

They arrived safely but felt shame at facing Grandmother Song without the rest of the family. They had no idea whether the rest were dead or alive.

In Chuncheon, meanwhile, my grandmother, Song Inhyeon, heard on the radio that troops were fighting in nearby Cheorwon, just 15 miles away. The government urged residents to evacuate.

"She knew that the communists had my father on the top of their enemy list since he was a National Assembly candidate for Syngman Rhee's National Party, which meant that my father and my family would be either executed or taken political prisoners if they were in Communists' hands," Uncle Hank wrote.

With no time to pack or prepare provisions, my father recalls that they fled empty-handed, with just the clothes on their backs. With the roads to Seoul closed, they headed south, crossing the surging Hongcheon River and climbing the steep Taebaek mountain range on foot.

"It was a throng of people, all the way from Chuncheon over the mountain, the river, on foot," my father recalls.

It took them two full days to reach the town of Yeoju, about 40 miles away. Along the way, my father and his siblings relied on the generosity of villagers for food and shelter. Too weak to walk, my grandmother rode on the back of a family helper; none of them knew she was pregnant. From Yeoju, they continued onto Suwon, staying overnight at the home of a business associate. They caught the last train out of that city before rail lines were cut off.

In Yeongdong, there had been no news for days about what happened to the Chuncheon family. But on June 30th, there was a hopeful sign: a groundskeeper spotted someone waving a white cloth from a cargo train arriving at Yeongdong Station.

"Soon after, with the watch dogs barking loud, a bunch of beggars ... showed up," Uncle Hank wrote. "There they were, all nine of them, looking horrible, exhausted, but happy beyond description! We couldn't believe our eyes. It was like a dream."

The Lee family was reunited. Eventually, dozens of relatives from the Song clan descended upon their ancestral home, seeking refuge at the 99-room estate. (Only the king could have a home with 100 rooms, under Joseon Dynasty rules.)

But the respite was short-lived. As the North Koreans pushed southward, my grandfather and his older sons headed farther afield to look for safer accommodations for the family. They were cut off when the North Koreans captured Yeongdong on July 25, outmaneuvering the newly arrived U.S. forces.

At one point, my Uncle Yong-chong narrowly escaped death when U.S. soldiers trained their machine guns on him and other South Koreans in a bid to flush out communists suspected of hiding in their midst. The US attacks on civilians in the Yeongdong hamlet of Nogeun-ri were revealed in a Pulitzer Prize-winning investigative story about the Korean War massacre.

On another occasion, the family took in two thirsty, hungry American soldiers fleeing North Korean troops. Unable to tolerate the spicy Korean food, the Americans left to look for sustenance — and were likely taken prisoner or killed, my father says.

In Yeongdong, meanwhile, food became scarce, even for the well-to-do Songs. "There were so many of us that we had to leave. So many people to feed," my father recalls.

In late July, his mother decided to take the younger children to Okcheon, my grandfather's ancestral hometown, outside the central city of Daejeon. There, they sought refuge in the sarang-bang, one of the outer rooms, of a grand home in Okcheon said to have once belonged to the family.

Tragedy in Okcheon

Okcheon was a dangerous place to be in the summer of 1950. It was close to Daejeon, where UN troops had lost the Battle of Taejon in mid-July. On Aug. 25, Maj. Gen. William F. Dean, commander of the US Army's 24th Infantry Division, was taken prisoner by the North Koreans.

The US Army left behind trucks filled with firearms and bullets. "I got in and played with those guns that they left behind," my father recalls. But food was scarce. "You can't imagine. We had nothing, nothing to eat."

My grandmother came up with a desperate plan: She would send the older children back to Chuncheon on their own, in hopes that their house would still be standing, even though the city was occupied by the North Koreans.

One August morning, the children set out on foot. They walked for a full day, eventually finding a family willing to take them in for the night.

"We cried all night, all of us," my father recalls. "And then we decided: Well, if we're going to starve to death, we want to go back and die with Mom."

They returned to Okcheon to find their mother sobbing on the veranda. Gathering them in her arms, she told them: "If we die, we die together."

The dangers were not all found in the conflict. The older children knew to avoid the nuts from the ginkgo trees in the backyard, which can be toxic. But the youngest, Geun-jong, could not resist. The older children watched helplessly as the toddler began vomiting and then convulsed in the courtyard.

He was dead by morning. "What could we do?

Nothing," my father recalls.

Geun-jong's death plunged my grandmother into grief. Very much a traditional Korean woman, she never allowed herself to be seen without her hair in a bun. But when her youngest died, she let her hair down.

It was a sight that sparked panic in my father, then 10. "I saw her walking to the mountain in back [of the house], so I followed her for fear she was going to commit suicide," he recalls.

She returned safely after a respite in the mountains, to his relief.

Inchon and Beyond

In September 1950 came news of a daring amphibious assault by the US Marines at the port of Incheon west of Seoul. Gen. Douglas MacArthur's bold intervention, known as the Inchon Landing, allowed UN troops to regain control of nearby Seoul and push the North Koreans back up the peninsula.

My grandfather and his two older sons emerged from hiding and rushed to Okcheon.

"We expected our little Geun-jong to run out first to meet us, but he wasn't with the family. We quickly sensed something wrong, but nobody said a word," Uncle Hank wrote.

The family had buried Geun-jong without a funeral or tombstone.

"After a moment, my father broke the silence by saying that Geun-jong took all our misery and suffering with him, and left us alive and well through his sacrifice," he recalled. "We all cried, even my father had tears in his eyes, maybe more for losing the little brother GJ than for joy of our reunion."

They continued on to Seoul to find their home completely destroyed. Neighbors told them the North Koreans had seized the property and installed an anti-aircraft machine gun on the roof. A UN fighter jet obliterated both the gun and the three-story home.

The family's big house in Chuncheon had fared no better. The North Koreans had turned it into a regional headquarters, and it was destroyed in an air raid. My family lost everything in those first few months of war.

As the UN troops crossed the 38th Parallel and seized Pyongyang, the Lees began rebuilding their lives in Seoul. They thought the war would be over soon.

But in October 1950, the Chinese joined the war, cornering the US Army's X Corps with a sneak attack in Jangjin, North Korea, in what is known by the Japanese-era name as the Battle of the Chosin Reservoir. Encircling tens of thousands of UN forces in a brutal fight in late November and early December, Chinese troops forced them to retreat below the 38th

Parallel again – and retook Seoul. It was a dangerous time to be a young man in the South Korean capital.

One day, my father tells me, an uncle, who was a newly married veterinarian, stepped out of the house to run a quick errand. His wife later learned he had been seized by the North Koreans. Two other uncles, a physician and a diplomat, also disappeared. Both were leftists, my father recalls, and may have joined the North Koreans voluntarily, he says.

The family never saw or heard from them again.

The Rats of Busan

In January 1951, the Lee family fled south once again, this time during a bitterly cold winter and with a new baby, my Aunt Young-shim, in tow. They bribed their way onto a freight train and sought refuge in the southwestern port city of Busan along with nearly all of Seoul.

All ten of them squeezed into one ramshackle room that served as kitchen, living room and bedroom until my grandfather could find them a proper house. "Terrible" is how my father remembers it, with everyone in the shantytown sharing an outdoor toilet where the waste spilled into the street.

When asked about that room, both my father and my Uncle John said the same thing: "Rats everywhere." They even dropped from gaps in the ceiling.

Eventually, their father was able to secure a more comfortable home in Busan. My father remembers holding his own among the local Busan bullies at elementary. Uncle Hank wrote about tuning into the Armed Forces Network radio to learn English, and falling in love with the music of Frank Sinatra, Nat King Cole, Eddie Fisher, Tony Bennett and Doris Day. He was already on his way to becoming an American.

As the fighting continued, representatives from North Korea and China began meeting in July 1951 with counterparts from the United States and the United Nations to negotiate a cease-fire. Those talks stretched on for two years until an armistice agreement was signed on July 27, 1953.

News of a truce arrived on my father's 13th birthday. The Lee family left Busan and returned to a devastated, demolished Seoul. Amid the rubble, the Lees resettled in Changseong-dong, next to Gyeongbok Palace in Seoul, and focused on rebuilding their lives.

New Lives, New Americans

With South Korea in ashes, my grandparents set their sights on sending their sons off to America to be educated. Uncle Hank left for Dudley, Massachusetts, the following year, and John and YC soon followed him to the United States. Eventually, five of my grandparents' eight surviving children, including my father, became US citizens, raising the next generation here as Americans.

We children of those Korean War "peasants" became doctors, journalists, economists, professors, musicians, fashion designers and CEOs, making our family story not just a Korean War memory but also an American tale. We are proof that the defense of South Korea was worthwhile. (For a truly astounding Korean-American tale, read The Great Leader and the Fighter Pilot, by Blaine Harden.)

Today, my father's story has come full circle. After 30 years in the United States working as a neurologist, he returned as a U.S. citizen to a South Korea that he did not recognize in 1991. He has since regained South Korean citizenship, making him and my mother dual nationals. They live not far from Chuncheon, the city of his birth, though the wreckage of the house that the North Koreans occupied has long since made way for downtown office buildings.

My father turns 80 this year. And it is only now that I have asked him what happened when the Korean War broke out 70 years ago.

It is an awkward conversation, so many years late. In

many Korean families like mine, we rarely discussed the war growing up, choosing instead to bury the most difficult memories and to focus on moving forward. That's how Korean families survive.

But my work as a journalist has taken me to enemy North Korea dozens of times. So I think constantly about the Korean War and the impact it still has on geopolitics in Northeast Asia today.

It is not often that we mark the start of a conflict; we typically celebrate their end. However, this is a war that has not formally ended. There has been no peace treaty. To call it a Forgotten War is ironic, because it is a conflict that is very much alive — in North Korean ideology and propaganda, inside the Demilitarized Zone, and in the faltering diplomacy between North Korea and the United States.

To forget about this war is irresponsible; remembering is the key to understanding. We cannot negotiate peace and stability without understanding and resolving the conflicts and resolutions of the past.

For me, remembering what happened in 1950, and in the years that followed, is essential to understanding what shaped my father's life — and, ultimately, mine.

Jean H. Lee is Director of the Hyundai Motor-Korea Foundation

Center for Korean History and Public Policy at the Wilson Center, and a former AP Seoul bureau chief who also opened the news agency's bureau in Pyongyang.

17. Memories of a Young Boy

Hak Joo Choi (최학주, Spouse of Yer-ae Choi)

Translated by Yer-ae K. Choi (김여애)

In 1950 I was attending a subsidiary of Miari Elementary School located in Ui-dong where Grandfather lived. It was a one-room school, where a teacher named Chu taught only first and second graders. Beginning in third grade, I had to walk 20 ri (5 mi.) to the main school, so my family decided to move to Samseon-gyo where my father lived. My father was then a professor at Seoul National University Hospital. In May of that year, my sister Dong-joo and I transferred to Kyo-dong Elementary School, she as a first grader and I as a third grader.

June 25th was a Sunday, so there was no school. When I woke up, I heard the grownups whispering that a war had broken out along the 38th Parallel. My father left hurriedly for the hospital. Half a month would pass before he could return to Ui-dong. He said he couldn't leave the injured patients at the hospital and that there were too few doctors for too many patients.

After waiting for a few days for my father, my mother seemed to give up the idea of fleeing and decided to head for Ui-dong. Clutching our little bundles that my mother packed, my sister and I followed my mother, crossing the Miari Pass, heading toward Uijeong-bu. On the sides of the streets, we saw demolished tanks, half-burned trucks, and corpses covered with straw mats. My mother told us not to dawdle and hurried us along. She tried to shield my little sister by lifting one end of her long skirt. I just walked, thinking to myself, maybe this is what war is like. I didn't feel scared at all.

Everything was quiet at Ui-dong. No tanks, no corpses. It was exactly the same as when I had left it two months before. Nothing in my room had changed either. There was my folded bedding, my low desk, my comic books, my copy of The Thousand Chinese Characters, a wall clock, a top, a box of cards, a bag of marbles—everything was there. Outside, I saw the sled, the slightly deflated soccer ball, my shepherd dog Meri, and several brown, white, and black chickens that followed me around. Everything was there.

Then it happened midsummer that year. Bored out of my mind, I didn't know what to do with myself. I remember it was a hot and muggy day.

In the shade, I am playing with Meri under the front steps. Through the open windows, I hear the boisterous laughter of women ironing bed sheets with charcoal-filled irons. All of a sudden, the laughter stops. I look up, and see five or six North Korean People's Army soldiers stepping into the front yard through the open gate. My mother emerges from the inner room, and after hurriedly slipping into her shoes on the stone step, goes down to the yard and stands in front of the soldiers. My dog Meri tries to pull away and jump on the soldiers, but I hold her back, pulling on her leash and collar with all my strength.

My mother inquires in a quiet voice on what business they have come. The soldier in charge doesn't answer. Instead, he orders everyone present to step down to the front yard. My mother explains in a still quieter voice that there are only two elderly parents in the inner room. The soldier is insistent and threatens to enter the room himself unless everyone comes out promptly. Then, with his boots still on, he jumps onto the hall floor. At that very moment, we hear Grandmother's voice from the inner room, "Just a moment, dear, I'll be out shortly."

Everyone stays still, including the soldiers. The only movement comes from Meri who still struggles to get free of my hold. One of the soldiers gives Meri a threatening look and begins to take his rifle down from his shoulder. I get up quickly, trying harder to hold on to Meri. Everyone—my mother, the women who had been ironing, the soldiers—turns towards me.

I tell Grandmother, who has just come out of inner room, "Grandma, I'll go get Grandpa." Grandmother says, "Yes, go get Grandpa, dear."

I know Grandfather is in his study at the little house. Getting up, I again pull hard at Meri, but she pulls back harder. I give her a kick, shouting that we have to go to Grandfather quickly. Meri doesn't listen, and I begin to sweat. I know she will calm down once we pass the rear gate—but then I see Grandfather entering by it. Someone must have alerted him already.

Everyone is standing in a row between the *Jangtokdae* (a raised area in the yard where large jars of food are kept) and the low trees. Red peppers are drying on a large straw mat in the yard. I begin to worry that the soldiers will trample on the mat with their dirty boots. With her tongue hanging out in the summer heat, Meri has now quieted down a little. One of the soldiers, who looks a little brighter than the others, starts to examine everyone's hands. First he looks at the backs of our hands and then turns them over to examine the palms. He doesn't say anything while doing this. After the second in line, the rest voluntarily show the soldier both sides of their hands.

Grandfather is standing at the end of the row. Now it is his turn. As the soldier examines his hands, he suddenly palpates Grandfather's palms with his own fingers. With a disapproving look, he shouts at Grandfather, "YOU, comrade, are a reactionary!" Grandfather seems a little taken aback and responds, "Huh...?"

Everyone is familiar with the word *reactionary*, but no one seems to know what it means exactly. Grandfather must have known, but he simply puts his hands down to his sides and looks at the soldier without saying anything. The soldier doesn't say anything either. Then he looks away and asks for water. He orders his men to rest in the shade.

Grandfather and I head back to the little house. On the way, I ask, "What is a 'reactionary,' Grandpa?" Grandfather doesn't seem to have a ready answer. ". . . I have no idea."

This is what I remember of the day when the soldiers of the North Korean People's Army visited our house in Ui-dong.

That summer, Ui-dong was unusually quiet. By September, American bombers were flying over Ui-dong, but they left it alone. The children my age sang 'Jangbaeksan' (the North Korean anthem) instead of 'Donghaemul' (the South Korean anthem), oblivious to what was happening in Seoul. Our food was running low, and we often had gruel instead of rice. Grandfather was happy that we had a good harvest of potatoes that summer. In mid-September, my mother, my sister, and I returned to Samseon-gyo, and were relieved to find some food left in the house. On September 29, the news of Seoul's repatriation reached us.

Grandfather Escapes Abduction to the North

During 6.25, many prominent public figures, such as Yi Kwang-su, Chung In-bo, and An Chae-hong, were abducted to the North, but Grandfather escaped abduction. Some have theorized that Grandfather's escape was possible due to the consideration shown by Hong Myung-hi, who was then a high-ranking member of the Military Committee of the Chosun Labor Party in North Korea. I know this is not the case because neither Yi Kwang-su, whom Hong had held in high regard, nor Jeong Inbo, who was Hong's in-law, went to the North voluntarily. Others surmised that Grandfather eluded abduction because his youngest son, Han-gum, held a relatively high position in the City Labor Party in Seoul at that time. I know this is not the case, either.

About a week after the visit by the North Korean soldiers, one of whom called Grandfather a "*reactionary,*" my father came to Ui-dong from Seoul. It was around the middle of July. As in countless villages across South Korea, many things were happening in my village. My house was the only house in the village with a tile roof, and most of the villagers were tenant farmers attached to Grandfather's estate. Many of them were illiterate, totally unaware of what was happening in the outside world. It was they who chose my father as president of the village's People's Committee. My father was a big-hearted, sociable man. He joked effortlessly with the villagers, and often drank *makgeolli* (rice wine) with the tenant farmers. It was these farmers, along with Kyung-man, the son of the village shaman, Ahn, the warehouse truck driver, and Chung, owner of the village general store, who banded together and decided that my father, 'a man of education,' should be the president. As vice-president, they chose Chu, who was then a teacher at the Ui-dong subsidiary of Miari Elementary School.

About a month later in mid-August, my father and a young man named Won were sent away to join the Righteous Volunteer Army led by the North Korean Army. At the time, a fierce battle was raging near the Nakdong River perimeter near Busan, and every able man under the age of 35 was mobilized. My father was 36 at the time, but he had to go anyway. I remember going to the open field at Donam Elementary School with my mother to give him some money and rice balls before he left.

The day before his departure, my father had asked Chu to take care of Grandfather. Chu had promised that he would gladly look after the "family of Choe Nam-sun." Chu's wife graduated from Kyunggi Girls' High School in the same year as my mother. My mother was aware of the family's financial difficulties and quietly helped them in any way she could. One day, Chu's wife came to see my mother and warned her that the People's Committee had been discussing "the Choe Nam-sun question," so he should flee immediately.

Taking the house servant Yi with him, Grandfather escaped to a nearby mountain where he stayed in a tiny cottage owned by the village shaman. He had with him only a bag of potatoes and a Buddhist sutra he had been reading. When the soldiers from the People's Committee came for him the next day, my mother told them that he had gone to a temple to attend a service. Chu and his wife had kept their promise to my father and saved Grandfather from abduction.

My Aunt Is Murdered and My Mother Is Beaten

With the Repatriation of September 28, 1950, members of the Korean Youth Corps, under the pretext of national security, appeared in Ui-dong, just as they did in other villages throughout Korea. The head of the Ui-dong Youth Corps, who had been running for a

National Assembly seat prior to 6.25, accused Chu and his wife of being "Reds" for several reasons: one having to do with the whereabouts of my father, the former president of the People's Committee; another reason related to Third Uncle's going to the North with the retreating North Korean Army.

As the investigation progressed, one of the police officers who had kept Third Uncle under watch before the war was found murdered. The Youth Corps accused Chu of being the killer, and he, along with his wife and three children, were openly executed near a stream in the village. The men who pulled the triggers had been Chu's students. His only 'crime' was that he had been chosen by the uneducated villagers as vice president of the People's Committee. If he had been a true 'Red,' he would have gone North, just as Third Uncle had. The three murdered children were even younger than I was at the time.

Sam-ung, my best friend in Ui-dong, witnessed the execution. Afterwards, he told me, "They had to kill the children because Mrs. Chu was trying to cover them with her body." As if Sam-ung had anything to do with the killings, I screamed at him, "WHY DID THEY HAVE TO KILL MRS. CHU?!"

6.25 was like that. Children, barely ten years old, talked about killing and dying as if they were mundane events. Grownups with guns and rifles acted like children, and children fought like the grownups.

My father, who had been president of the People's Committee, was put under arrest order. The Korean Youth Corps believed that the reason Grandfather had not been abducted was because Third Uncle had used his influence as an important member of the City Labor Party. There were many unfounded theories flying about. Grandfather went to Seoul and stayed at the house of Sim U-sup's daughter, waiting for things to quiet down.

Then one day the Korean Youth Corps came to the house and arrested my mother. I was arrested, too, but was let go because of my young age. My mother was detained for over a month and beaten for information about the whereabouts of her husband, her brother-in-law, and her father-in-law. Grandfather, on learning of his daughter-in-law's plight, immediately paid a visit to Cho Byung-ok, then Minister of Interior, and demanded her prompt release. My mother was released after a month-long detainment in Dongdaemun police headquarters on charges of 'sheltering collaborators.

Grandfather's tragedy didn't end there. His daughter, Han-ok, the mother of six of his grandchildren, was murdered in Seoul by the retreating North Korean soldiers, and her husband was abducted to the North.

Han-ok, who had graduated from Tokyo Teachers' College, was a mother and housewife, living a quiet life, with little interest in public affairs. Three months after the breakout of 6.25, Grandfather had no information on the whereabouts of any of his three sons and knew not even whether they were alive or deadThe Burning of Grandfather's Library

On January 4, 1951, the Chinese Red Army invaded Korea. Grandfather fled to Busan on a military truck arranged by Sin Suk-u, a childhood friend who was then Korean Ambassador to Taiwanese China. In Busan, Grandfather, as adviser to the Committee for the Compilation of Korean Naval History, was deeply involved in the commemoration project for Admiral Yi Sun-sin. After the repatriation of Seoul in May of 1951, he asked my father to get the books he needed for the project from his Ui-dong library. With the assistance of the Commander-in-Chief of the Korean Navy, my father was able to reach Ui-dong by way of Incheon. On arrival, he saw that Grandfather's library, with its collection of 170,000 books, had burned to the ground. A month before, during the Chinese Spring Offensive in April, the American bombers had napalmed Ui-dong.

Grandfather took great pains to safeguard the collection. To him, it was not a personal possession, but a repository of Korea's cultural heritage for which he was a mere caretaker. The reason he moved out to rural Ui-dong was that he felt the location would provide a safe haven from the destructive powers unleashed by the Pacific War. But Ui-dong had turned out to be no haven after all; instead, it became his library's burial ground. On hearing that his book collection had burnt to the ground, he wrote a long piece of sijo, probably the longest as well as the most heart-rending in his entire collection. Here are some excerpts:

Ten years ago I tried my best to hide it from harm,
Only to prepare its burial ground ten years later.
I can but chuckle at how my toils have all been for naught.

One ordeal arrives right on the heels of another.
Mercilessly scorched by the flaming train of ordeals,
I learn to endure, remembering the old tale of Job.

Every piece of paper, every letter, I gathered with my soul.
Now they're all gone up in flames, but their spirits remain. Each one lives on, untouched, in my memory.

The Return to Seoul and My Father's Death

In the spring of 1952, Grandfather returned to Myo-dong in Seoul where Grandmother stayed behind. In

June of the same year, my mother, my sister, and I also returned to Seoul and together we waited for my father to join us after tying up loose ends in Busan.

Then one afternoon, the postman came and handed me a telegram, which I gave to Grandfather, who was then conversing with some guests. After reading the telegram, he told the guests, "Forgive me, but I need to take care of some family matter." When the guests had left, he turned to me and said softly, "Dear, go get Mommy."

Once the family had gathered and taken their seats, Grandfather told Grandmother, "It looks like something has happened to Han-in."

That was all he said. Grandmother and my mother must have understood, but my sister and I didn't know what those words meant. Soon Grandmother broke into loud sobs, and my mother gathered my sister and me into her arms. I saw tears in my mother's eyes. My father had suffered a cardiac arrest that morning and died suddenly in Busan. For Grandfather, the chain of tragedies that 6.25 unleashed had not yet come to an end. On July 31, 1952, he wrote this sijo in his black notebook:

For a glorious stroll down life's wide road,
He had everything, seeming to lack nothing.
Who'd have thought it would be so short?

Once again, Heaven raises his sharp whip.
I, a ne'er-do-well, have little use for you,
Why, why do you test me with such bitter trials?

The ice that falls and the fish that gets away seem
big, So goes the saying, but now I find much truth in
it. I know not what to do should this grief persist.

My eldest son, Han-in, had exceptional inborn talent
and extraordinary spirit. I loved him with all my heart.
He passed away a year ago in Busan, where he lived an
unsettled life during 6.25. His life dreams are but
flowers that fell before their full bloom. He not only
excelled in athletics such as figure skating and
volleyball, but was also an outstanding medical doctor.

After my father's death, Grandfather recited, with me
sitting beside him, the Buddhist Prayer to the Goddess
of Mercy for three hours every morning for 49 days. I
was 12 years old then.

Hak Joo Choi earned his doctorate from Tufts, and worked at
various US pharmaceutical companies including American
Cyanamid and Block Drug,
Yer-ae K. Choi was an editor at several publishing houses such as
Macmillan, Scholastic, and Harcourt.